THE LIVERPOOL YEAR

Kenny Dalglish

with
John Keith

of the Daily Express

Willow Books
Collins
8 Grafton Street, London W1
1988

Willow Books
William Collins Sons & Co Ltd
London · Glasgow · Sydney · Auckland
Toronto · Johannesburg

First published 1988
Text © Superstars Ltd 1988
Pictures © Bob Thomas 1988

British Library Cataloguing In Publication Data
Dalglish, Kenny
The Liverpool year.
1. England. Association football. Clubs.
(Association football). Liverpool Football Club
I. Title
796.334′63′0942753

ISBN 0−00−218337−4

Designed by Sackville Design Group Ltd, Hales Barn, New Street,
Stradbroke, Suffolk IP21 5JG
Set in Century Schoolbook and Univers by Sackville Design
Group Ltd and Bookworm Typesetting, Manchester
Printed and bound in Spain by Cronion S.A., Barcelona

Contents

Acknowledgements

In presenting my diary of Liverpool's year I would like to thank all the players and every single member of the club's staff and directors for their contributions, as well as our supporters who have been magnificent by backing us in even greater numbers. Liverpool is a very successful club but it has never forgotten its roots and has retained a family atmosphere which encompasses everyone from the chairman to the fans on the Kop.
I also wish to place on record my deep appreciation of the support I have received from my own family, which increased during the season when my wife Marina presented us in February with a lovely baby daughter Lauren.
My thanks also go to John Keith of the *Daily Express*, who chronicled this account of our season and who also had his family extended during the compilation of this book by the arrival of a baby daughter Isobelle.
The superb photography in the book is by Bob Thomas who has 'lived' with Liverpool FC since last summer, has been a regular visitor to our dressing-room yet has remained admirably unobtrusive.

Kenny Dalglish
May 1988

CLOSE SEASON

Friday, 15 May, 1987:   As I flew from Tel Aviv to Heathrow with the Liverpool players at the end of a marvellous chapter in the club's history, and at the prelude to a brand new one, I took time to reflect on changes in the team and how these would affect our prospects next season.

Our friendly match against Israel's national team at the Ramat Gan Stadium was Ian Rush's last appearance in a Liverpool jersey and I consider it a privilege to have played alongside him and been associated with him as manager.

It is going to be an unforgettable summer for Rushie, with his marriage to Tracey coming up in July before he starts a new life and a new phase of his career in Italian football with Juventus. I am sorry to lose him. Which club and which manager wouldn't be? But we have had a year's notice of his departure after his £3 million transfer was signed and sealed in Turin last June, which has given us valuable time to plan ahead for next season.

Since we knew Ian Rush was leaving the media have been filled with speculation about how we are going to replace him. But we intend to make more than one new signing, in addition to John Aldridge who we bought from Oxford last January. We will start from scratch when the new season kicks off in August and then the responsibility for scoring goals and trying to win matches will be shared by everyone in the team.

▶ *Two-goal Ian Rush and myself in jubilant mood after our historic 3-1 Wembley win over Everton in 1986.*

As Rushie himself has said on several occasions, losing one player has never halted or hampered Liverpool in the past and he does not expect it to do so now, even though his own goal-scoring output has been phenomenal. He deserves all the credit and plaudits that have been showered upon him and, because of the quality and quantity of the goals he has scored, he is an individual singled out for special attention by the media. But Liverpool have never achieved anything without that essential element of teamwork which has become our trademark during years of unprecedented success. And so it must stay. It is the foundation for all we do at Anfield and it has been like that since I signed from Celtic ten years ago.

▼ *Ian Rush's second goal against Everton at Wembley made it 3-1 and with it we clinched the FA Cup and League double in 1986.*

At least we know the men we want to sign in time for next season – Peter Beardsley of Newcastle and Watford's John Barnes. When you go shopping it always helps to know what you want to buy. You might not find it or get it, but at least you start out with a purpose and something in view.

Beardsley and Barnes have been in our sights for some time. If we can sign that pair, following last season's arrival of Aldridge, I'll have the three new players I want. That is my judgment and I am prepared to take my chances on it.

We have already agreed a £900,000 fee for Barnes in talks we had with Watford manager Graham Taylor two months ago and John has promised us a decision next month. We have also contacted Newcastle about Beardsley. Now all we can do is await developments and hope our moves are successful.

People have asked me why John Aldridge has been picked for only two games since we paid Oxford £750,000 for him. Well, the answer is that I have selected what I considered the best team for each match we have played. John scored in each of the two matches he has started for us – the League game against Southampton in February, when his header past Peter Shilton brought the only goal of the game, and our final First Division match at Chelsea last Saturday which we drew 3-3. So perhaps I was wrong not to play him more often. But his turn will almost certainly come and I am glad we have got him. He was a player we were interested in for quite a while because he has the greatest single attribute in football – the ability to score goals.

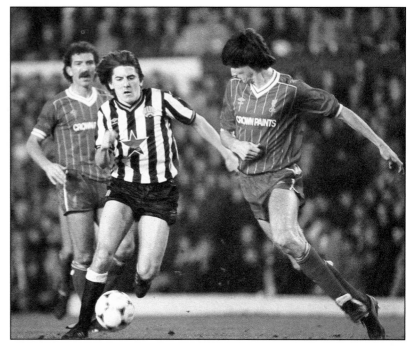

When Oxford told us he was available, we were delighted to do business and sign him. By one of those quirks of fate John, a born-and-bred Scouser, was turned down as a youngster by Liverpool before joining non-League South Liverpool and then Newport en route to Oxford. For John, who stood on the Kop as a lad cheering on the likes of Ian St John and Roger Hunt, it has been a long way round to 'come home' and realize the dream shared by thousands of fans – actually to become a Liverpool player.

John resembles Ian Rush in appearance and I hope the media do not start labelling him the 'new Rush'. That would be ridiculous. As I have said, no player has been – or will be – signed by me to replace Rushie. He will be signed to help Liverpool FC to success next season.

Last season, after our historic League title and FA Cup double in 1986, we finished runners-up to Everton in the First Division and to Arsenal in the Littlewoods Cup. A major trophy eluded us but I do not feel under any pressure because of that. In fact, apart from being a little wiser and that much

◀ *Three players captain Alan Hansen will not have to worry about in future because they are on our side now. They are pictured here playing for their former teams: John Barnes for Watford, with Alan in opposition; Peter Beardsley for Newcastle; and John Aldridge for Oxford.*

▲ *A sentimental return for John Aldridge to the famous Kop, where he used to stand as a youngster cheering on Liverpool in the days of Roger Hunt and Ian St John.*

▶ *A double celebration as Bob Paisley and I savour the moment Liverpool won the Double.*

more experienced in the ways of management, I feel no different now than when I was honoured by being offered the job in the aftermath of the Heysel Disaster two years ago. Throughout my career in the game I have endeavoured to do my best as a player and a manager. If you do that you can do no more. And if all of us at Anfield do that, we have got a chance.

My thoughts were interrupted when the seat belt signs were switched on – we were coming in to land at Heathrow.

Saturday, 16 May: Cup Final day in England and Scotland. I have been working for the BBC at Wembley and managed to tip the winner as Coventry beat Tottenham, and the odds, with a 3-2 victory after extra time. North of the border, St Mirren beat Dundee United, also after extra time.

Tuesday, 9 June: I returned from a family holiday in Spain last Saturday. Our chief executive Peter Robinson had phoned me there with the news that John Barnes wants to join us. A meeting had been arranged for today.

A welter of statements in newspapers and on radio and

◀ *My last game for Liverpool before becoming manager, face-to-face with Massimo Briaschi of Juventus on the tragic occasion of the 1985 European Cup Final in Brussels.*

television over the past weeks have been saying that John has kept us waiting since we first agreed a fee with Watford in March. But John's meeting with us is taking place just 24 hours after the 8 June date we had settled on with Watford manager Graham Taylor – so how has he kept us waiting?

Since our talks with Watford, Graham Taylor has left to take over as manager of Aston Villa. However, the agreement between the clubs, made before the end of John's contract, was not affected and we arranged a motorway rendezvous with him halfway between Watford and Liverpool. John had thought over his future, as he told us in March he intended to do and which he had a perfect right to do. He assured us he was not responsible for newspaper stories linking him with Arsenal and Tottenham, and said he was keen to sign for Liverpool.

We are delighted that having weighed up his future he has decided to come to Anfield. Our motorway meeting was concluded with no problems and we set off back to Merseyside to hold the Press conference announcing his signing.

▶ *England signing No.1: John Barnes becomes a Liverpool player.*

The fact that John happens to be the first Black player Liverpool have bought was something that had not crossed my mind until it was pointed out to me. At Liverpool we are not concerned with race, creed or the colour of a person's skin. The only thing that matters to us is whether a player we would like to sign is available and keen to join us. And in John's case those things applied.

Some people seem surprised that a player of such obvious individual skill as John should come to a club like Liverpool whose success has been based on teamwork, but I think he will complement us and vice versa. I have admired him for a long time. We know he has the speed and ability to go past people and not only is he one of the best, if not *the* best crosser of a ball in British football but he will contribute a great deal to the team effort. He is never shy of going back to help out in defensive situations and, of course, at set pieces he can be a menace to the opposition.

John has always impressed us as an opponent, playing for Watford; watching him, we have always enjoyed and admired his performances. There is no doubt in my mind that he has the attributes to improve our team; and, in turn, he can learn things here that will benefit him.

Thursday, 2 July: Our hopes of signing Peter Beardsley soared today. His club, Newcastle United, contacted us and Peter travelled down to Merseyside for talks. I met him at a

▼ *This is home for the new boys...the green grass of Anfield.*

▲ *The summer of '87 was unforgettable for Ian Rush. A new career with Juventus awaited him and he married his fiancée Tracey.*

Southport restaurant in the company of his wife Sandra, my wife Marina, our chairman John Smith and Peter Robinson, and we had an enjoyable evening.

Unlike John Barnes, Peter has another year of his contract to run, but Newcastle had stated that they were prepared to sell him and Peter said he wanted to come to Liverpool. Everything was agreed, but the completion of the transfer has been unavoidably delayed because Peter has personal business to conclude with Newcastle.

Friday, 3 July: Peter returned to the Northeast while my wife Marina and I were among the guests at Ian Rush's wedding. He married Tracey Evans at St Mary's Church in their home town of Flint, North Wales. His Liverpool room-mate Ronnie Whelan was best man and crowds of people gave the couple a great send-off. I hope they have a happy marriage and wish them the best of luck in Italy.

Tuesday, 14 July: Peter Robinson rang me at home yesterday with the good news that everything had been sorted out between Beardsley and Newcastle, and that he would be coming down to sign for us at Anfield today.

Peter arrived and, in front of whirring cameras and dozens of media people, signed the transfer forms to make him Britain's most expensive player at £1.9 million. That is a lot of money. But we have got a very good player and we believe in providing the best for our supporters, because they deserve no less. A club's real assets are on the field of play and, as my former Scotland boss Tommy Docherty once said, at the end of the day any money a club has really belongs to the supporters.

Our chairman John Smith told the Press conference: 'This is the first time in the history of Liverpool – maybe in the history of any club – that two current England players have been signed in such quick succession.'

As with John Barnes, we have admired Peter for some time. Although he scored only five League goals last season, it was Newcastle's worst for some years and they finished in seventeenth place. Peter contributed to a fair proportion of the eleven goals scored by their leading marksman Paul Goddard, and without those Newcastle could have been relegated.

Peter's goal figures for his previous seasons at Newcastle were impressive. In 1983-84 – his first season with them after returning to England from Vancouver Whitecaps – his League total of twenty was bettered at the club only by Kevin Keegan who scored twenty-seven. And in the next two seasons following their promotion to Division One, Peter was their leading

League marksman with seventeen and nineteen goals respectively.

I have no doubts about his scoring potential and I certainly have none about his creative ability, which has been exemplified in his England partnership with Gary Lineker. His experience of big occasions at international level is another factor that will hold Peter in good stead as a Liverpool player.

Unfortunately, our fans will have to wait to see our new players make their home debuts because, only hours after Peter's signing ceremony, Peter Robinson announced that our first two home games of the new season – against Charlton and Derby – have been postponed because of a collapsed sewer underneath the Kop. There is a possibility, too, that the following Anfield fixture, against Watford, will also have to

▼ *John Aldridge, Peter Beardsley and John Barnes in Munich before our opening 1987 pre-season game against Bayern. The match revived memories of a previous game in the Olympic Stadium against the West German champions in the 1981 European Cup semi-final second leg. Bayern's Calle Del'Haye is pictured tackling me in the fifth minute of the match and I had to go off with damaged ankle ligaments. But the team did brilliantly to knock out Bayern and we went on to win the trophy by beating Real Madrid in Paris.*

◄ England signing No.2: Peter Beardsley and I shake hands at his transfer Press conference.

be rearranged. That would mean starting with three away games, but we must simply accept the situation as something beyond our control. And, as somebody once said, if something is worth having, it is worth waiting for.

▲ The collapsed sewer under the Kop kept us waiting for our first home game of the season.

BACK INTO ACTION

Tuesday, 21 July, 1987: Tomorrow we will fly to Munich for our return to match action at the start of a pre-season programme lasting almost three weeks and spanning five countries – West Germany, Denmark, Sweden, Norway and Scotland. I realize it is a bit longer than some tours we've had at this important conditioning stage of the year, but for the new players and, therefore, for us in general, it will be invaluable. Being away from home for a few weeks helps players to get to know each other properly and certainly quicker than they could possibly do at home. It helps them become a unit.

Our latest signings John Barnes and Peter Beardsley have done pre-season training sessions with us; and although John Aldridge and Nigel Spackman were with us last season this is their first pre-season at Liverpool. By preparing for and starting the new season as Liverpool players they will be totally accustomed to life at Anfield and feel the full benefit of our training methods.

▼ *Training with some of the players at the start of our pre-season tour in West Germany. Left to right: Steve Nicol, John Barnes, me, John Aldridge and Alan Hansen.*

These methods are largely unchanged, but for one or two minor adjustments, since I first joined the club ten years ago, and probably since the days of Bill Shankly's management which began in 1959. Bob Paisley, Joe Fagan and now myself have followed in the manager's seat, but the club's training ideals have remained constant – to make players as fit as possible in our attempts to bring success to the club.

All our training takes place at our Melwood training centre and players work hard in the sessions, which are designed to cover every aspect of their performance: stamina, finishing, passing and also supporting and finding positions when they are without the ball, which is the majority of the time during an actual match. The sessions are demanding – about one and a half hours each morning once the season is under way – but what players do away from the club and training ground is every bit as important. They should conduct their lives responsibly and follow a reasonable diet, remembering at all times that they are professional footballers who should wear the Liverpool FC shirt with pride.

Since I became manager a little more than two years ago I have had the best of all worlds: I have had access to the great wisdom of Bob Paisley – my first boss at Anfield and the most successful ever in the English game – and, on the training ground, I have been able to tap into the knowledge and expertise of coaches Ronnie Moran and Roy Evans. It was agreed and announced when I took the job that Bob, also a club director, would act as consultant for my first two seasons as manager. That period has now expired officially. But I know that if ever I need his shrewd advice I have only got to ask. So really nothing has changed.

▶ *Here is a fine assembly of football wisdom and knowledge. A picture taken almost twenty years ago shows (left to right): the late Bill Shankly, my first Anfield boss Bob Paisley, Ronnie Moran, my managerial predecessor Joe Fagan and Reuben Bennett.*

◀▼ *Ronnie Moran at work in training with goalkeeper Bruce Grobbelaar, watching me set off on a run and then shouting instructions to the players with John Aldridge well within earshot.*

▲ *My number's up! This was in Rome during the 1984 European Cup Final when I was replaced by Michael Robinson. The No. 7 board went up again during our pre-season tour.*

Bob has been with the club since 1939 and is totally committed to Liverpool. And so are Ronnie and Roy who, between them, have served this club for more than sixty years as players and backroom men. They have been tremendous. From the moment I was offered the job I wanted them to stay. I didn't know too much about the coaching and training side of the game and, if I'd had to choose two men for the job, it would have been these two. It must have been difficult for them suddenly to switch from shouting at me in training sessions to calling me boss. But they have never complained and we work in total harmony. I realize they can educate me and, at the same time, if I ask for a little thing to be done, it is done. Teamwork counts as much behind the scenes as it does with players on the field.

Wednesday, 22 July: We travelled from Anfield by coach to Manchester Airport to board a flight to Munich for tomorrow's match against West German champions, and last season's European Cup finalists, Bayern.

Unfortunately, injury has deprived us of another player. Shortly before our departure, Danish international Jan Molby was diagnosed as having broken a bone in his foot, the result of a tackle in training on the very spot where he took a blow playing in Denmark's European Championship game against Czechoslovakia in June. So we had to leave him behind, along with our three long-term casualties – midfielder Kevin MacDonald, who fractured his left tibia and fibula in our League game at Southampton last September, left-back Jim Beglin, who broke his left leg in the Littlewoods Cup tie at Everton in January, and versatile Mark Lawrenson, who suffered a ruptured Achilles tendon in our home League game against Wimbledon in March. They are making good progress but we have set no comeback targets for any of them and the same will apply to Jan.

Nigel Spackman has a knee injury but I have included him in the tour squad. It is good news, too, that goalkeeper Bruce Grobbelaar and Steve Nicol are also in the squad after regaining fitness during the summer from their injury problems of last season. Steve has not played a first-team game since December, having suffered problems arising from a hernia operation last summer. And Bruce missed the final four games of last season after breaking his right elbow at Manchester United in April.

I have also included eighteen-year-old Belfast-born midfielder Jimmy Magilton in the tour party. Like striker John Durnin, who travelled on last year's pre-season tour and is

starting to show one or two impressive touches in the reserves, I think Jimmy can only benefit from being with us. The full seventeen-man squad is: Bruce Grobbelaar, Barry Venison, Steve Nicol, Gary Gillespie, Alan Hansen, Gary Ablett, Ronnie Whelan, Craig Johnston, Steve McMahon, Jimmy Magilton, John Barnes, John Wark, Nigel Spackman, Paul Walsh, Peter Beardsley, John Aldridge, and myself.

After a delay of several hours at Manchester Airport due to technical difficulties we arrived in Munich and checked into our hotel in the afternoon.

Thursday, 23 July: Tonight's match against Bayern, a testimonial for Dieter Hoeness in the Olympic Stadium, was one of the most difficult we could have picked to open our pre-season programme. Not only are Bayern one of Europe's

▲ *Peter Beardsley battles with Pele – the nickname for Bayern's guest player Ayeu Adedi – during our pre-season game.*

BAYERN MUNICH 3

LIVERPOOL 2 (Aldridge, Barnes)

Friendly   23 July

LIVERPOOL

Grobbelaar	SUBSTITUTES:
Gillespie	Wark
Venison	Ablett
Nicol	Magilton
Whelan	Dalglish
Hansen	
Beardsley	
Johnston	
Aldridge	
Barnes	
McMahon	

foremost clubs, but they had the advantage of already having played several games. However, the whole object of the pre-season tour is to condition players physically and mentally, so the match was immensely valuable from that viewpoint.

The signing of John Barnes to play wide on the left meant that Ronnie Whelan could move inside to play a central midfield role, with Peter Beardsley partnering Aldridge up front.

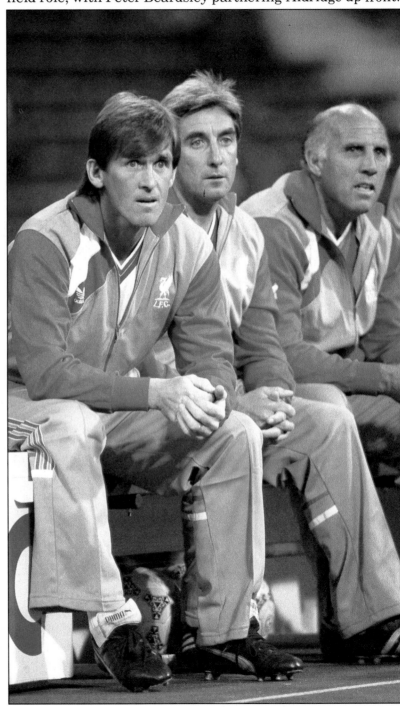

▶ *On the bench at Munich's Olympic Stadium: me, Roy Evans and Ronnie Moran.*

Bayern's greater sharpness was evident as they took a 2-0 lead by half-time with goals from West German international Lothar Matthaus and Hoeness; their new signing Jurgen Wegmann made it 3-0 after 71 minutes. But John Aldridge cut that deficit with a far-post header from a John Barnes cross two minutes later – his third goal in only his third start for us. In the 83rd minute he provided the pass for Barnes to score on his debut. We lost 3-2 but, as we also hit a post and Bayern played a host of substitutes while we used none, we put up a very creditable display against a total of about eighteen Bayern players on the night.

Sunday, 26 July: We left Munich yesterday after a day off on Friday. We flew to Aalborg in Denmark, via Copenhagen, for today's match against Chang Aalborg, which was part of the club's 75th anniversary celebrations.

▼ *Get out of that one! Bayern's Helmut Winklhofer in a tangle, trying to cope with the talents of John Barnes.*

One of the aims of pre-season tours is to give as many players as possible as much action as possible. So I brought Paul Walsh and Gary Ablett into the team, with Steve Nicol and Steve McMahon switching to the bench.

We showed good attacking play against our Danish Third Division opponents who had been reinforced by a sprinkling of guest players. After nine minutes we took the lead, when Paul Walsh turned on to a Barnes corner and crossed for John Aldridge to head in. Then Walsh was brought down after 37 minutes for a penalty that provided Aldridge with his second goal of the match and his fifth in only the fourth game he has kicked off in a Liverpool jersey. It was a good outing for Walshie, too, because his pass three minutes before half-time allowed Whelan to put us 3-0 up with a well-struck shot.

In the second half, we sent on Jimmy Magilton, Steve Nicol and John Wark to take over from Barry Venison, Whelan and Aldridge. John Barnes continued his happy start to his Liverpool career with our fourth goal and his second in as many matches.

Tuesday, 28 July: Yesterday we flew from Aalborg back to Copenhagen and then travelled by road for today's match against Broenshoej.

Keeping to the objective of pre-season games, I put myself in the starting line-up to remind my legs what matches are like! Nigel Spackman also had his first taste of pre-season action. Both Nigel and I had a 75-minute stint before John Aldridge and Ronnie Whelan came on as substitutes. A Steve Nicol goal gave us a 1-1 draw.

CHANG AALBORG 0	
LIVERPOOL 4 (Aldridge 2 inc. 1 pen, Whelan, Barnes)	
Friendly 26 July	
LIVERPOOL	
Grobbelaar	SUBSTITUTES:
Gillespie	McMahon
Venison	Nicol
Ablett	Wark
Whelan	Spackman
Hansen	Magilton
Walsh	Dalglish
Aldridge	
Johnston	
Beardsley	
Barnes	

BROENSHOEJ 1	
LIVERPOOL 1 (Nicol)	
Friendly 28 July	
LIVERPOOL	
Grobbelaar	SUBSTITUTES:
Gillespie	Aldridge
Venison	Whelan
Ablett	Beardsley
Nicol	Johnston
Hansen	Magilton
Dalglish	
McMahon	
Walsh	
Spackman	
Barnes	

◀ *Craig Johnston and I in a discussion during a training stint on our pre-season tour.*

# AUGUST

August is the month when the curtain goes up on the League championship; but we have four games to play before our opening First Division fixture at Arsenal.

Saturday, 1 August, 1987:   For the fourth match of our pre-season tour we met the Danish club Vejle and I went back on the bench after coming off in the previous game.

I have already been asked by the media on this tour whether, at the age of thirty-six, I am considering officially hanging up my boots. The question is being asked, I think, because my playing contract expires next summer. But I have told them that I will know when the time comes for me to pack up. Nobody will have to tell me. And Dalglish the manager will pick Dalglish the player only when he feels it is in the best interests of Liverpool FC.

I am keeping fit – or trying to – and I feel no different about my playing future than I did when I took on the job of player-manager. It will all depend on how I feel, not on my birth certificate. And that is how it should be. I knew what I was taking on when I accepted the job even though I didn't – and couldn't possibly – have known the intricacies of management because I had never done it before.

Similarly, I don't know what it would be like to be manager without also being a registered player because I have known no different since becoming player-manager in 1985. That is why I have been so fortunate in having people like Bob Paisley, Ronnie Moran and Roy Evans to help me on the various aspects of management that are new to me.

The lads put on an impressive show this afternoon but the Danes, often defending desperately, restricted us to a 3-0 win, all our goals coming in the first half from Johnston, Beardsley and Aldridge. Aldridge's goal was a header, as three of his four tour goals have been, and as were the first of his two League goals for us last season. Overall, he has scored six times in five starts for us. During the summer I telephoned him to put his mind at rest following unfounded newspaper speculation that we were going to sell him. I assured him that he had a future here and I am very pleased at the way he has started for us.

Steve McMahon took a knock on the knee during the match, so John Wark went on as substitute for the last half-hour; and Nigel Spackman had another taste of the action by replacing Gary Gillespie. We flew back to Copenhagen after the match.

VEJLE 0

LIVERPOOL 3 (Johnston, Beardsley, Aldridge)

Friendly   1 August

LIVERPOOL

Grobbelaar	SUBSTITUTES:
Gillespie	Wark
Venison	Spackman
Nicol	Walsh
Whelan	Magilton
Hansen	Dalglish
Beardsley	
Johnston	
Aldridge	
Barnes	
McMahon	

Tomorrow will be another day of travel. We will go by coach to Copenhagen Airport – our fifth visit in nine days! Then we will take a flight to Oslo in Norway and transfer by coach across the border into Sweden for Monday's match against Karlstad.

Monday, 3 August: We scored another 3-0 win against the Swedes, which is very encouraging because we experimented with just three at the back and rested captain Alan Hansen – Nigel Spackman, Gary Gillespie and Steve Nicol were the men in defence.

With big 'Jockie' Hansen absent from the starting line-up I gave the captaincy of the team to Ronnie Whelan. Although Ronnie is still only twenty-five he is one of our most experienced players, having signed for us as a youngster from the Dublin club Home Farm eight years ago and forced himself through to win a regular place and collect a host of honours.

KARLSTAD 0	
LIVERPOOL 3 (Walsh, Beardsley, Aldridge pen)	
Friendly 3 August	
LIVERPOOL	
Grobbelaar	SUBSTITUTES:
Gillespie	Wark
Spackman	Hansen
Nicol	Magilton
Whelan	Venison
Walsh	Dalglish
Beardsley	
Johnston	
Aldridge	
Barnes	
McMahon	

▶ *Republic of Ireland international Ronnie Whelan is now an experienced Liverpool campaigner. He switched to a central midfield role after our signing of John Barnes to play wide on the left.*

He has also gained plenty of international experience with the Republic of Ireland and shown impressive versatility for Liverpool. I have selected him at left-back, right midfield, left midfield and his new position in the centre. He has even been used up front, and has responded well wherever he has been asked to play. We always know what we will get from Ronnie – maximum effort and no little skill. He takes great pride in his performances and playing for Liverpool.

The game was goalless at half-time, but we scored in the second half through Paul Walsh – who came off so that I could have another taste of action – Peter Beardsley and a John Aldridge penalty. John Wark did another substitute stint for Steve McMahon.

Thursday, 6 August: Still based in Oslo, we were in action tonight at the famous Bislet Stadium, scene of so many athletics world records, where we met the Norwegian club Valerengen.

We started the match once again deploying just three at the back – Alan Hansen, returning to the side after his one-match rest, Barry Venison and Steve Nicol. Although we reached half-time 2-1 in front, the three-man defensive system did not work as well as in the previous game. We changed it after 20 minutes with John Wark dropping back to play alongside Hansen and performing well in that role.

Steve McMahon came on at half-time in place of Peter Beardsley and I replaced John Barnes after 62 minutes. Our 4-1 win was notable for a hat-trick by John Aldridge, a feat that is always a source of satisfaction no matter what the level of competition or the standard of the opposition. One of Aldridge's three was a penalty and his overall total for Liverpool is now ten goals in seven games he has started, including eight scored on this tour. Long may he continue to be so prolific!

Sunday, 9 August: After flying home from Oslo on Friday, I travelled straight up to Scotland to watch Celtic, our opponents today, play Morton. Our players were able to spend one night at home before hitting the road again yesterday for today's match against my old club – the Tommy Burns Testimonial at Parkhead.

The only goal of the game went to us, thanks to a magnificent strike by Ronnie Whelan from almost thirty yards.

Peter Beardsley was in action yesterday for the Football League against the Rest of the World in the centenary match at Wembley, so I gave him a rest today and picked Paul Walsh

---

VALERENGEN 1

LIVERPOOL 4 (Aldridge 3 inc. 1 pen, Walsh)

Friendly   6 August

LIVERPOOL

Grobbelaar	SUBSTITUTES:
Venison	McMahon
Nicol	Gillespie
Johnston	Magilton
Whelan	Spackman
Hansen	Dalglish
Beardsley	
Walsh	
Aldridge	
Wark	
Barnes	

▼ *Jimmy Magilton, our teenage Belfast-born midfielder, had a taste of life with the first team squad when he travelled on our pre-season tour.*

to play alongside John Aldridge up front. I couldn't resist the temptation to have a taste of the action against my old club, and went on for Walsh in the 56th minute with Peter Beardsley taking over from Aldridge after 77 minutes.

We could have won by a comfortable margin – the lads produced good football and created quite a few chances. However, Ronnie's first-half goal settled it. This concluded our seven-match pre-season programme in which we were unbeaten since our opening game against Bayern, when circumstances contributed to the outcome.

Each player has greatly improved his fitness level and I am very pleased with the overall performance. My only regret is that young Jimmy Magilton had the opportunity of only 33 minutes of action as a substitute on this tour. But I hope and believe that the experience of being with the first team squad travelling around Europe for almost three weeks will stand him in good stead and pay dividends in the future.

Now we can think solely about the opening of the League programme because it is our next match – a trip to Arsenal, one of the other fancied championship contenders and the club that beat us at Wembley in the Littlewoods Cup Final last April.

▶ *A wave to the fans from the dug-out on the season's opening day at Highbury.*

▶ *Half an hour to go until kick-off: the Highbury gates are already closed on a bumper 54,000-plus crowd.*

CELTIC 0

LIVERPOOL 1 (Whelan)

**Tommy Burns   9 August
  Testimonial**

LIVERPOOL	
Grobbelaar	SUBSTITUTES:
Gillespie	Beardsley
Venison	Spackman
Nicol	Ablett
Whelan	Wark
Hansen	Dalglish
Walsh	
Aldridge	
Johnston	
Barnes	
McMahon	

◀ *A trip down memory lane for me and a taste of action rolled into one as I have a run-out against my old club Celtic in the Tommy Burns Testimonial match at Parkhead, our final pre-season game.*

▶ *Our directors at Highbury for the opening League game. I don't know about it being 'the perfect match', as announced by the advertisement hoarding, but it certainly lived up to many people's expectations.*

THE PER

▶ *Bruce Grobbelaar wins this battle of the goalmouth at Highbury.*

Friday, 14 August: Yesterday, just forty-eight hours before the big kick-off, we were given the news that our third home game – our 31 August fixture with Watford – has been postponed because heavy rain has delayed repair work to the collapsed sewer under the Kop. So that means that Charlton, Derby and Watford all have to be rearranged and that our home supporters must wait until the game against Oxford on 12 September to see the team and the new players in action.

It must be a big disappointment to them and I know it is a disappointment for the players, especially the new lads who were so looking forward to playing at Anfield. But there is nothing we can do about it and we will just have to do our best in the games as they come along. We will still have the same number of matches to play whatever order they come in.

To fill in one of our blank weekends, caused by work to the Kop, we received permission today to play Atletico Madrid in Spain a week on Sunday.

At my Anfield Press conference about tomorrow's game at Arsenal some media representatives seemed surprised that I have named the team and substitutes the day before the match. I told them that I have been able to do so because – the long-term casualties excepted – everyone is fit. I already had a good idea of the side I wanted to select at Highbury but you daren't look too far ahead because injuries can often wreck your plans. Fortunately, though, we emerged from our pre-season programme with no additional major injuries.

ECT MATCH

▶ *An anxious moment during the Arsenal match. Roy Evans and I watch as Peter Beardsley takes a knock.*

ARSENAL	LIVERPOOL
First Division	**Highbury**
15 August	**54,703**

ARSENAL 1 (Davis)

LIVERPOOL 2 (Aldridge, Nicol)

ARSENAL	LIVERPOOL
Lukic	Grobbelaar
Thomas	Gillespie
Sansom	Venison
Williams	Nicol
O'Leary	Whelan
Adams	Hansen
Rocastle	Beardsley
Davis	Aldridge
Smith	Johnston
Nicholas	Barnes
Hayes	McMahon
SUBSTITUTES	
Groves	Walsh
Caesar	Spackman

Saturday, 15 August: The sun shone at Highbury as we started the season and we knew we were in for a difficult game. Some people described this as our day of judgment in the aftermath of Ian Rush's departure and the arrival of John Barnes, Peter Beardsley and John Aldridge, who had started only two previous senior games. It was nothing of the sort; although you could say that every day is a day of judgment in this game. It was simply the first match of another long and testing season and our only concern this afternoon was trying to win three points.

Talking of new players, Steve Nicol almost falls into that category. He played at left-back today for his first competitive match since before last Christmas, and when you welcome back someone after so long out of action it is almost akin to having a new player. It was certainly great from our viewpoint to have Steve available again because he can fill a number of positions and do a good job in each one.

Just nine minutes into the game we took the lead through John Aldridge, who beat John Lukic with a header after a move involving our two other new boys John Barnes, who supplied the cross, and Peter Beardsley. But Paul Davis headed Arsenal level just eight minutes later and, in all honesty, the game could have gone either way on a very warm afternoon.

It was still 1-1 with five minutes to go when we sent on Paul Walsh for Beardsley, who was feeling the effects of a couple of kicks he had received. With just three minutes left, Steve Nicol celebrated his return with a headed winner from the edge of the box after Tony Adams had headed away a Barnes free kick.

Naturally, we are delighted to have started the season by collecting three points from a difficult away fixture but now, because of work to the Kop, we will have to wait a fortnight before our next First Division action.

Wednesday, 19 August: To keep us ticking over we flew to Dublin to play an Irish Olympic XI at Lansdowne Road. We gave Nigel Spackman an outing at right-back in a side that produced a 5-0 win.

The sizeable crowd generated a wonderful atmosphere. Ronnie Whelan weighed in with a goal in his native city to open the scoring, which was followed by a John Aldridge penalty, a Peter Beardsley goal and two from Paul Walsh after he had replaced Craig Johnston.

Saturday, 22 August: On our way to Melwood for training yesterday the team bus was involved in a minor collision with a double-decker bus; the players had to complete the journey on foot. Fortunately, no big problems beset us today as we flew to Madrid, even though we went via Barcelona, the city at the centre of an air traffic control dispute.

We arrived in Madrid only slightly delayed, to prepare for tomorrow's match against Atletico which precedes Everton's game against Real here on Wednesday. This week could see another double step towards English clubs being readmitted to Europe, and tight security measures have been drawn up. European football does have a different flavour, but this is the third season we have been banned from UEFA competitions and I have adjusted to and accepted the situation. Obviously, we hope to be back in again as soon as possible. Until then the only thing players can do – and I mean at every club – is to conduct themselves in the best possible manner on the field and leave the negotiations for a re-entry to the football authorities.

It is an intriguing point to consider that more than half our squad on duty at Arsenal have had little or no experience of European football at club level. John Barnes and Paul Walsh have made half a dozen appearances each, Gary Gillespie, Steve McMahon and John Aldridge four apiece, while Barry Venison, Peter Beardsley and Nigel Spackman have not made a single club appearance in Europe between them. So nobody can claim that they have suffered by missing out on European

IRISH OLYMPIC XI 0	
LIVERPOOL 5 (Whelan, Aldridge pen, Beardsley, Walsh 2)	
Friendly 19 August	
LIVERPOOL	
Grobbelaar	SUBSTITUTES:
Spackman	Walsh
Wark	Gillespie
Nicol	Irvine
Whelan	Venison
Hansen	Dalglish
Beardsley	
Aldridge	
Johnston	
Barnes	
McMahon	

football! Conversely, others say that European competitions are the losers by not having English clubs and players of such ability participating in them.

On the subject of a return to European competition, I believe that it would be extremely difficult for any club to control or be responsible for its own fans. What is to stop anybody hellbent on fomenting trouble from wearing a Liverpool scarf, an Everton scarf or any club's colours and posing as a supporter of that club when they are nothing of the sort? We can only hope that, if and when English clubs are allowed back into Europe, the destructive hooligan element has been defeated.

ATLETICO MADRID 0

LIVERPOOL 1 (Wark)

**City of   23 August
Madrid Cup**

LIVERPOOL

Grobbelaar	SUBSTITUTES:
Gillespie	Walsh
Venison	Wark
Nicol	Spackman
Whelan	Dalglish
Hansen	
Beardsley	
Aldridge	
Johnston	
Barnes	
McMahon	

Sunday, 23 August: Our match against Atletico in the Vicente Calderon Stadium was a valuable exercise for us and our 1-0 win – thanks to that expert European marksman John Wark who scored in the 73rd minute – was a great result.

I think we spoiled the party for the home fans, who had turned out to see a new Atletico team built by new manager, Cesar Menotti, and new club president, Jesus Gil. Recent arrivals to that team include Paulo Futre from European Cup winners Oporto and former Athletic Bilbao defender Andoni Goicoechea. However, it was one of *our* new signings, John Barnes, that played a starring role, and we left the stadium with the City of Madrid Cup.

Friday, 28 August: Alan Irvine, the forward we signed from Falkirk last November, has returned to Scotland by signing for Dundee United in a £100,000 transfer deal. Alan did not have much of an opportunity to play here at first-team level, and did not start a senior game for us. However, one of his four substitute appearances will not be forgotten quickly by the club or by our supporters. It was against Everton at Goodison Park in the Littlewoods Cup quarter-final last January.

We lost Jim Beglin with a broken leg after 25 minutes, and Barry Venison replaced him. Then at half-time Steve McMahon had to withdraw with groin trouble. Alan was pitched into the cup tie and a boiling derby atmosphere. But his response and that of the rest of the players in the resulting major team reshuffle was magnificent, and we got our reward when Ian Rush scored the game's only goal six minutes from the end. Thanks for your efforts Alan and best wishes for the future.

Saturday, 29 August: During the week we received encouraging news about Mark Lawrenson; he had been given the go-ahead by the club surgeon to start his comeback in the

A team against Chester today – his first game of any kind since sustaining a ruptured Achilles tendon against Wimbledon last March. His period at the FA's National Rehabilitation Centre at Lilleshall proved beneficial in pushing along his recovery programme.

The same team and same two substitutes named for our opening game at Arsenal were on duty at Coventry today. Steve Nicol, who clinched that late victory at Arsenal, gave us a great start by putting us ahead after 19 minutes. He scored again five minutes into the second half, his third goal in our first two League games. John Aldridge's penalty made it 3-0 after 52 minutes – his thirteenth goal in twelve starts – and Peter Beardsley scored a well-taken fourth. Cyrille Regis hit a memorable consolation goal for the FA Cup holders a minute from time, an indication that the entertainment level was maintained right to the end.

COVENTRY CITY	LIVERPOOL
First Division	**Highfield Road**
29 August	**27,637**

COVENTRY 1 (Regis)

LIVERPOOL 4 (Nicol 2, Aldridge pen, Beardsley)

COVENTRY	LIVERPOOL
Ogrizovic	Grobbelaar
Borrows	Gillespie
Downs	Venison
McGrath	Nicol
Kilcline	Whelan
Peake	Hansen
Bennett	Beardsley
Gynn	Aldridge
Regis	Johnston
Speedie	Barnes
Pickering	McMahon

SUBSTITUTES:	
Houchen	Walsh
Phillips	Spackman

◀ *Heads it's mine! John Barnes in a midair tussle with Coventry's Dave Bennett.*

We have got to be pleased with six points from our first two games, both away, and Coventry manager John Sillett said our performance was probably the finest he has ever seen in the First Division. But we're not getting carried away. A very heart-warming aspect of the afternoon was the way in which the large number of Liverpool fans who travelled to Highfield Road gave tremendous vocal support to John Barnes and Peter Beardsley. Both players told me afterwards that it gave them a great lift and that they are now bursting to make their Anfield debuts as Liverpool players. But we've got one more away-day before that . . .

▼ *The fans pack into Highfield Road to watch our match at Coventry. Our supporters were there in their thousands to give the players, especially John Barnes, tremendous vocal encouragement.*

▼ *Bruce Grobbelaar races out to deny Coventry's David Speedie a scoring opportunity.*

SEPTEMBER

Saturday, 5 September, 1987:   Today we played our third consecutive away League match of the new season, on a wet, heavy pitch at West Ham. We had to make our first team change because Craig Johnston was unfit after suffering a groin injury in training. Nigel Spackman came in to take over on the right of midfield and played his part in a very impressive performance. Unfortunately it was one in which our finishing did not match the rest of our play and the final result was a draw, 1-1.

▲ *John Barnes pursued by West Ham substitute George Parris.*

We had plenty of chances to win the match. One of our many penetrating moves ended when George Parris brought down Steve McMahon, giving John Aldridge the opportunity to put us 1-0 up from the penalty spot after 52 minutes. It was John's fourteenth goal in thirteen starts for us all told, and it makes no difference whatsoever that penalties have helped him reach that total. They are part and parcel of the game, they have to be earned by your play, and then they have to be put away. John is proving what a good penalty-taker he is.

We should have had the game wrapped up, but in the 73rd minute Alan Hansen's attempted back pass to Bruce Grobbelaar was cut out by Tony Cottee, who rounded Bruce and scored West Ham's equalizer – a rare mistake by Alan and one that the media have latched on to. They seem to have overlooked the fact that, for once, we had made mistakes in our forward play by not making our many chances count.

During the course of the game we switched John Barnes to the right flank with Nigel Spackman moving to the left. It was a variation we tried just to attempt to win the game. We are still unbeaten but it was frustrating to come away from Upton Park with only one point.

The good news is that Mark Lawrenson came through his third comeback outing in the A team against Everton with no problems; he will now have a reserve game against Derby on Tuesday. However, Craig Johnston's injury means he must withdraw from the Football League squad due to meet the Irish League in Belfast on Wednesday.

Saturday, 12 September: The big day – our first home game of the season, against Oxford United. The team's previous performances and the way in which the new players have

WEST HAM UNITED	LIVERPOOL
First Division	Upton Park
5 September	29,865

WEST HAM 1 (Cottee)

LIVERPOOL 1 (Aldridge pen)

WEST HAM	LIVERPOOL
McAlister	Grobbelaar
Stewart	Gillespie
McQueen	Venison
Strodder	Nicol
Martin	Whelan
Brady	Hansen
Ward	Beardsley
McAvennie	Aldridge
Ince	Spackman
Cottee	Barnes
Robson	McMahon

SUBSTITUTES:	
Dickens	Walsh
Parris	Wark

◀ *Skipper Alan Hansen is not happy with himself after a rare mistake set up Tony Cottee's equalizer for West Ham. But our forwards missed chances at the other end.*

settled in so comfortably were encouraging signs. Today the team had the chance to show our home supporters what they are capable of on their own territory; they had already enjoyed the tremendous backing of the large number of our fans who had travelled to away games.

For the first time this season Mark Lawrenson was fit enough to be included in our original sixteen-strong squad. However, with Craig Johnston still ruled out with his groin trouble I decided on an unchanged team. I also chose the same two substitutes, Paul Walsh and John Wark.

The atmosphere was terrific, as was the football itself. Only 13 minutes into the match, John Barnes made a run and crossed for John Aldridge to arrive at the far post and to score his first goal at the Kop, where he once stood as a boy cheering on past Liverpool teams. It was a great moment for John and for us. The fans, needless to say, were equally delighted.

We went two up after 37 minutes thanks to more magic from John Barnes. Beardsley's free kick was played to Whelan for Barnesie to blast left-footed past Peter Hucker. The fans went wild – they had witnessed John's great talent. The only disappointing thing is that we failed to add further goals in the second half. But we won and conceded nothing.

I was impressed, and not for the first time, by Ray Houghton's performance in Oxford's midfield. He looks a fine player and is a good competitor.

LIVERPOOL	OXFORD UNITED

First Division	Anfield
12 September	42,266

LIVERPOOL 2 (Aldridge, Barnes)

OXFORD 0

LIVERPOOL	OXFORD
Grobbelaar	Hucker
Gillespie	Slatter
Venison	Dreyer
Nicol	Shelton
Whelan	Briggs
Hansen	Caton
Beardsley	Houghton
Aldridge	Foyle
Spackman	Whitehurst
Barnes	Hebberd
McMahon	Saunders

SUBSTITUTES:	
Walsh	Langan
Wark	Phillips

◀ *The Anfield curtain goes up on the League season as Nigel Spackman and Oxford's Ray Houghton tussle for midfield possession.*

▶ *The long wait is over for us and the Kop as a big crowd packs into Anfield for our first home League game, against Oxford. This match marked the Anfield debuts of new signings Peter Beardsley (right) and John Barnes.*

LIVERPOOL	CHARLTON ATHLETIC
First Division	Anfield
15 September	36,637

LIVERPOOL 3 (Aldridge pen, Hansen, McMahon)

CHARLTON 2 (Crooks, Walsh)

LIVERPOOL	CHARLTON
Grobbelaar	Johns
Gillespie	Humphrey
Venison	Gritt
Nicol	Peake
Whelan	Shirtliff
Hansen	Miller
Beardsley	Milne
Aldridge	Stuart
Spackman	C. Walsh
Barnes	Mackenzie
McMahon	Crooks
SUBSTITUTES:	
Walsh	Williams
Lawrenson	Pender

Tuesday, 15 September: Charlton were the second team to visit Anfield; and, although they were without a win, we could not afford to take any chances. I told the players – and the media – that we could improve on Saturday's display by sustaining that first-half performance through the full 90 minutes. The match turned out to be a marvellous evening's entertainment and a great advertisement for the game.

We found ourselves behind after just eight minutes when Garth Crooks – who scored the goal here in March 1985 that gave Tottenham their first Anfield win for seventy-three years – flighted the ball over Bruce Grobbelaar, who had come off his line. But within two minutes we were level: Charlton skipper Peter Shirtliff fouled John Aldridge to concede a penalty, which John put away in his usual composed style.

Nobody watching the match would ever have guessed that Charlton were down at the wrong end of the table, propping up the First Division. Their football was sparkling and there were thrills and spills in both goalmouths.

A magnificent strike by Colin Walsh from a thirty-yard free

kick put Charlton 2-1 in front after 59 minutes and we sent on
Mark Lawrenson as substitute for Nigel Spackman. It was
Mark's first senior action since his Achilles injury last March
and his appearance released Steve Nicol to switch from left-
back to right midfield. It was from Nicol's cross that Alan
Hansen headed a rare goal for our 71st-minute equalizer.
Well done, skipper – your timing couldn't have been better! It
was Hansen's first goal in a competitive match for us since
scoring at Coventry in May 1984.

Two minutes later, we crowned a terrific fight-back: a long
forward pass from Ronnie Whelan sent Steve McMahon
through and he drew goalkeeper Nicky Johns off his line
before firing our winner into the Kop net. Going 2-1 down at
home is enough to give anyone palpitations. But our lads then
proceeded to show their best football – the way they moved the
ball around from man to man was better than I have seen for
some time. Charlton must also be applauded for coming here
with a positive approach, for wanting to play and doing it in a
highly commendable way.

▲ *A timely goal from Alan Hansen (No.6) brings our equalizer.*

▶ *Weather-beaten! Charlton goalkeeper Nicky Johns, a lone figure in an Anfield downpour.*

◀ *John Aldridge tussles with Charlton's Paul Miller.*

Sunday, 20 September: Our first appearance on live television this season was at Newcastle in front of the BBC cameras. Media attention has been focused on Peter Beardsley's return to his native Tyneside to face his former club – and on the home debut of Francisco Ernandi Lima da Silva, the Brazilian who prefers to call himself Mirandinha.

It was a bold decision by Newcastle to sign him. Every transfer is a calculated risk but with a foreigner, especially a non-European, that risk is even greater. The extra factors of acclimatization, environment and the rigours of an English season have to be considered. Mirandinha has started well, scoring both goals in last week's 2-2 draw at Manchester United. His appearance today, and Peter's, undoubtedly added something extra to an already attractive fixture.

We decided to keep the side that had finished our game against Charlton in such breathtaking style. Mark Lawrenson started a match for the first time since March and Steve Nicol – Chico as we call him – was on the right of midfield, with Nigel Spackman and Paul Walsh the substitutes.

It proved to be quite an afternoon for Steve Nicol who stood out as the star of an entertaining team performance. John Barnes combined with Peter Beardsley in the 21st minute to send in a cross that deflected off John Anderson for Nicol to open the scoring. We went two up in 38 minutes when Barnesie's header down from Barry Venison's cross gave John Aldridge his chance to make it seven successive matches in which he has scored – one game more than the best sequence Ian Rush put together for Liverpool. We are not really interested in statistics of this nature and I doubt if it is high on

NEWCASTLE UNITED	LIVERPOOL
First Division	**St James Park**
20 September	**24,141**

NEWCASTLE 1 (McDonald pen)
LIVERPOOL 4 (Nicol 3, Aldridge)

NEWCASTLE	LIVERPOOL
Kelly	Grobbelaar
McDonald	Gillespie
Anderson	Venison
McCreery	Nicol
P. Jackson	Whelan
Roeder	Hansen
Stephenson	Beardsley
Wharton	Aldridge
Goddard	Lawrenson
Mirandinha	Barnes
Hodges	McMahon

SUBSTITUTES:	
D. Jackson	Spackman
Thomas	Walsh

▲ A half-time discussion with referee Keith Hackett following Steve Nicol's disallowed goal at Newcastle.

▲ Steve Nicol collects his second goal at Newcastle.

◄ Peter Beardsley, on his return to Newcastle as a Liverpool player, facing the double challenge of Glenn Roeder and Peter Jackson.

Aldridge's list of priorities. He – like us – is just happy to score.

A couple of minutes before half-time, we put the ball in the net again: Nicol curled it superbly over goalkeeper Gary Kelly, but we were desperately unlucky to see it chalked out for offside. Fortunately, though, we did not have to wait long for another that did count and, fittingly, Steve Nicol was the scorer, three minutes after the interval. Peter Beardsley, underlining his unselfish talent as a creator and provider, supplied the final pass.

Despite our domination of the game, Mirandinha impressed me with his speed and close control. His chances of proving an asset to Newcastle – and the First Division – appear very good. One of his runs resulted in a Newcastle penalty in the 61st minute, when referee Keith Hackett decided that Gary Gillespie had fouled the Brazilian. A harsh decision perhaps, but the referee's word must always be final. Neil McDonald scored from the spot to make the scoreline 3-1.

Five minutes later we restored our three-goal advantage thanks to a great goal by Steve Nicol which clinched his hat-trick and his sixth goal of the season. He ran on to John Aldridge's pass and chipped the keeper brilliantly. The final score was 4-1, making us the only unbeaten team in the First Division. Although we are pleased with the way things have been going, we do not intend to fall into the trap of looking too far ahead, only as far as the next game.

Wednesday, 23 September: League football took a back seat today as we travelled to Ewood Park to meet Second Division Blackburn Rovers in the first leg of the Littlewoods Cup second round. Unfortunately, Gary Gillespie, who had suffered a calf injury at Newcastle and had been replaced by Nigel Spackman for the last 20 minutes, was still unfit, so Nigel continued at centre-back in an otherwise unchanged team, with Paul Walsh and John Wark the substitutes.

Earlier in the day one of our reserve centre-backs, Mark Seagraves, signed for Manchester City in a £100,000 move. It would have been wrong for us to stand in Mark's way because we could give him no guarantees about a first-team future at Anfield. Now, at the age of twenty, he has an opportunity to make his mark in League football and I wish him luck.

At Blackburn, Steve Nicol found the net again, after half an hour! His goal put us in the lead and was his seventh in as many appearances this season, equalling his previous best whole-season totals of 1983-84 and 1984-85. He scored three of his goals when playing left-back, and the last four in his role wide on the right. That just proves how valuable a player he is.

▲ *The boy from Brazil. Newcastle's imported star Mirandinha in the thick of the action with Gary Gillespie.*

BLACKBURN ROVERS	LIVERPOOL
Littlewoods Cup	Ewood Park
23 September	13, 924

BLACKBURN 1 (Sellars)

LIVERPOOL 1 (Nicol)

BLACKBURN	LIVERPOOL
Gennoe	Grobbelaar
Price	Spackman
Sulley	Venison
Barker	Nicol
Hill	Whelan
Mail	Hansen
Gayle	Beardsley
Reid	Aldridge
Curry	Lawrenson
Garner	Barnes
Sellars	McMahon
SUBSTITUTES:	
I. Miller	Walsh
J. Millar	Wark

▼ *All in a night's work at Ewood Park, Blackburn, during the second half of our Littlewoods Cup first-leg game. We went ahead through Steve Nicol's first-half goal, but Scott Sellars equalized four minutes after the interval and the reactions and expressions of myself, Ronnie Moran and Roy Evans tell their own story. In an attempt to break the deadlock, we sent on Paul Walsh and gave Peter Beardsley a rest for the last 15 minutes.*

A lot more chances came our way but unfortunately we failed to take them; and Blackburn tied the game up when Scott Sellars equalized with a lunging header after 49 minutes. In an attempt to win the match we sent on Paul Walsh for Peter Beardsley for the final 15 minutes. A goal proved elusive, however, and the last scoring opportunity fell to Blackburn when Grobbelaar was forced to save from Simon Garner. If we had accepted just a few of our chances the game would have been well won. Now it is all square going into the second leg.

Thursday, 24 September: Leeds United contacted me to express their interest in Ken de Mange, one of our reserve midfield players. Ken has developed as a player at Anfield since joining us as a teenager from Home Farm, the Dublin club that also sent us Ronnie Whelan. Unfortunately for Ken, his talents have never had a chance to express themselves at

first-team level. However, although he has not made a senior appearance for us in a competitive match, his abilities were underlined by his breakthrough at international level: he won his first cap as a substitute in the Republic of Ireland's 1-0 win over Brazil last May.

Leeds were keen to sign him, and when I told Ken he decided that for the benefit of his career he would like to take the opportunity of challenging for a first-team place at Elland Road. After travelling to Yorkshire for talks and a medical, Ken signed for Leeds to complete the deal and, naturally, he carries our good wishes.

The papers were full of the substitution made during the Blackburn match, reading things into Peter Beardsley's replacement by Paul Walsh that are just not there. We were simply endeavouring to use all our available resources on the night in an effort to win the match, and sent on one attacker for another. So why all the fuss? If they think there are any problems with Peter Beardsley they are well wide of the mark. We are delighted with him.

We are also delighted that Kevin MacDonald came through his first match action since breaking his leg at Southampton a year ago this week. Kevin made his playing comeback in an A team game at Chester and finished it with no problems. This will have been a marvellous booster for him but, all along, his attitude has been superb. Another piece of good news is that Craig Johnston also completed the match after being unavailable for the last five first-team games because of a groin injury. He will be in contention for a place in the League match against Derby next Tuesday.

◀ *Steve Nicol scoring our only goal in the Littlewoods Cup first leg at Blackburn.*

▶ *One for Aldridge's scrapbook: the goal that clinched his hat-trick against Derby.*

LIVERPOOL	DERBY COUNTY
First Division	**Anfield**
29 September	**43, 405**

LIVERPOOL 4 (Aldridge 3 inc. 2 pen, Beardsley)

DERBY 0

LIVERPOOL	DERBY
Grobbelaar	Shilton
Gillespie	Blades
Venison	Forsyth
Nicol	Williams
Whelan	Wright
Hansen	MacLaren
Beardsley	Sage
Aldridge	Gee
Johnston	Davison
Barnes	Gregory
McMahon	Callaghan
SUBSTITUTES:	
Walsh	Garner
Lawrenson	Cross

Tuesday, 29 September: Craig Johnston's return to fitness and Gary Gillespie's recovery meant I had a lot of players to choose from for tonight's match with Derby, and I knew how disappointed those who were left out would be. I decided to recall Craig to right midfield, with Steve Nicol reverting to left-back, Gary returning at centre-back in place of Nigel Spackman and Mark Lawrenson being squeezed on to the substitute's bench alongside Paul Walsh.

There was a tremendous crowd of more than 43,000, which is exceptional for a midweek match. The players had to beat not only Peter Shilton in Derby's goal but also a five-man visiting defence of Mel Sage, Paul Blades, Ross MacLaren, Mark Wright and Michael Forsyth – a compliment, no doubt, to the way we have been playing and the number of goals we have been scoring.

In the 21st minute, the team had a goal disallowed, which was a bitter experience for them considering the barriers they had managed to overcome. Wright was booked by referee George Tyson for bringing down Gary Gillespie on a surging run. At the free kick, Ronnie Whelan ran over the ball and John Barnes hit a magnificent left-foot shot that beat Derby's 'wall' and Shilton to fly into the top corner of the net. But our celebrations were short-lived: the referee, on the intervention of a linesman, disallowed the goal, maintaining that it should have been an indirect not a direct free kick. All I know is that our lads believed it was direct and took it accordingly.

▲ A disconsolate Derby goalkeeper Peter Shilton on the night he conceded four goals at Anfield. But it could have been worse for him – we had another one disallowed!

DIVISION ONE

	P	Home W	D	L	F	A	Away W	D	L	F	A	Pts
QPR	9	4	1	0	9	2	3	0	1	5	2	22
Liverpool	**7**	**3**	**0**	**0**	**9**	**2**	**3**	**1**	**0**	**11**	**4**	**19**
Chelsea	9	4	0	0	10	4	2	0	3	8	7	18
Nottm For	9	1	2	1	4	4	4	0	1	11	5	17
Tottenham ...	9	4	0	0	9	2	1	2	2	3	4	17
Man Utd	9	3	2	0	8	3	1	2	1	6	5	16
Arsenal	8	3	0	1	11	2	1	2	1	2	3	14
Coventry	8	1	1	2	3	8	3	0	1	7	4	13
Everton	9	3	1	1	8	3	0	2	2	2	4	12
Wimbledon ..	9	1	3	0	7	4	2	0	3	4	7	12
Oxford	8	2	0	1	8	7	1	2	2	3	7	11
Portsmth	9	2	2	1	7	8	0	2	2	2	10	10
Derby	8	1	2	2	3	4	1	1	1	3	6	9
Luton	9	1	2	1	5	5	1	0	4	5	9	8
Newcastle	8	1	0	3	4	8	1	2	1	5	6	8
Watford	8	1	2	2	2	5	1	0	2	3	5	8
Southmptn ..	8	0	2	1	3	4	1	2	2	8	9	7
Norwich	9	1	1	3	5	7	1	0	3	1	4	7
West Ham	8	1	1	2	3	5	0	2	2	4	6	6
Sheff Wed	9	1	1	3	5	8	0	2	2	4	9	6
Charlton	8	1	0	3	3	6	0	1	3	4	10	4

The team deserve a lot of credit for reacting so positively to that setback, and the players got their reward when Forsyth brought down Craig Johnston four minutes before half-time and John Aldridge beat Shilton from the penalty spot.

The second half was only two minutes old when Aldridge headed down Craig Johnston's cross for Peter Beardsley to score his first home goal at the Kop end. He received his rightful salute from the fans. But for some great saves by Shilton – who I can only once remember making a mistake against us, in the FA Cup tie at Nottingham Forest in 1980 – we would have been several goals ahead before the hour.

We made it three in the 69th minute when another penalty conceded by Forsyth – this time for a challenge on Barnes – was slotted home by Aldridge. His delight was obvious to everyone when he clinched his hat-trick in the 73rd minute after Craig Johnston had helped on Steve Nicol's cross. The final score was 4-0 – a deserved reward for some fine football.

England manager Bobby Robson, who watched the game, joined in the praise of our team performance and likened the display of John Barnes to George Best. I think it is difficult to make comparisons. We are happy at the way John is playing just as we are happy about the contribution of everyone who has appeared in the team so far – and I am sure our fans feel they have been entertained.

OCTOBER

LIVERPOOL	PORTSMTH

First Division | **Anfield**

3 October | **44, 366**

LIVERPOOL 4 (Beardsley, McMahon, Aldridge pen, Whelan)

PORTSMOUTH 0

LIVERPOOL	PORTSMTH
Grobbelaar	Knight
Gillespie	Swain
Venison	Sandford
Nicol	Fillery
Whelan	Shotton
Hansen	Gilbert
Beardsley	Horne
Aldridge	Whitehead
Johnston	Mariner
Barnes	Quinn
McMahon	Hilaire
SUBSTITUTES:	
Walsh	Ball
Lawrenson	Dillon

Saturday, 3 October, 1987: The team was unchanged, and we named the same substitutes Paul Walsh and Mark Lawrenson, for Portsmouth's first Division One visit to Anfield for thirty-four years. Again – just as in our previous game against Derby – we were confronted by five-at-the-back, with Portsmouth manager Alan Ball detailing Barry Horne to stick with John Barnes in a bid to stifle his menace. I am glad

▶ *An aerial duel between Portsmouth's Paul Mariner (left) and Gary Gillespie.*

to say that the players overcame this obstacle and achieved another 4-0 win, our second in five days. However, just as pleasing as the goals we are scoring is the fact that we have come through another match with a clean sheet.

Peter Beardsley put us ahead after half an hour and Steve McMahon made it two early in the second half. When Steve broke through again and was fouled by Lee Sandford two minutes later, John Aldridge took the opportunity to make it 3-0 from the penalty spot.

John Barnes's pass to Ronnie Whelan set up our fourth goal which Dusty – our nickname for Ronnie – struck past Alan Knight in the 71st minute. In the Press room after the game I was asked whether man-marking Barnesie reduced our effectiveness. I replied: 'You'd better ask every other manager in the First Division who has still to play us because we have overcome the problems Portsmouth presented us with and scored four goals.'

▼ *John Barnes challenges Barry Horne.*

What is most encouraging is that our twenty-four League goals so far have been spread among seven players, and it was interesting to hear Portsmouth forward Paul Mariner's after-match comments: 'We tried to shut down the Barnes-Steve Nicol partnership on the left because it's been so dangerous and I thought we did it quite well . . . Barry Horne did a great job. But Liverpool have such quality all over the park – they were slipping out at us all over the place. If you stop one of them you've got the rest to deal with and I don't know if anyone will be able to.' When opponents talk like this, all our players can take credit.

▼ It is the 89th minute of our Littlewoods Cup second leg against Blackburn at Anfield – John Aldridge's header gave us a 2-1 aggregate victory.

Tuesday, 6 October: Bobby Robson paid our squad another compliment yesterday by naming Steve McMahon and Craig Johnston in the England B squad to play in Malta next week. Both lads have played at England Under-21 level and I know

their aim is to win a full cap. The only way they will achieve this ambition is by performing well for us, so they are going about it in the right way.

Steve McMahon's groin injury ruled him out of tonight's return with Blackburn, which we went into level-pegging after the 1-1 first-leg draw at Ewood Park, so John Wark came into midfield to start his first match of the season. I did not expect Blackburn to play any differently – or any better – than they did in the first game. I knew they would try to make it difficult for us and keep it tight, and that is what happened.

They managed to keep us goalless longer than any other team this season and, with two minutes left, it was still 0-0. Then Peter Beardsley took a corner, John Barnes crossed and John Aldridge headed the winner, timed at 88 minutes 41 seconds. It might have been a late goal but it was well deserved. There are 90 minutes in a game and goals scored towards the

LIVERPOOL	BLACKBURN ROVERS
Littlewoods Cup	**Anfield**
6 October	**28,994**

LIVERPOOL 1 (Aldridge)

BLACKBURN 0

LIVERPOOL	BLACKBURN
Grobbelaar	Gennoe
Gillespie	Price
Venison	Sulley
Nicol	Barker
Whelan	Hendry
Hansen	Dawson
Beardsley	Mail
Aldridge	Reid
Johnston	Curry
Barnes	Garner
Wark	Sellars

SUBSTITUTES:

Walsh	Ainscow
Lawrenson	Millar

▶ *Two on to one: the Blackburn pair David Mail (left) and Simon Garner are tested by this burst from Peter Beardsley.*

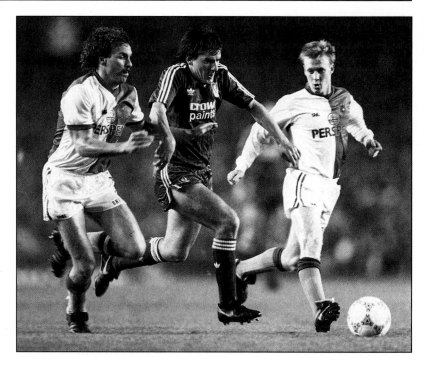

end are just as valid as those scored early on. We also kept another clean sheet – our third in a row – and if you do that you always have a chance.

We dominated the game to such an extent that the only save Bruce Grobbelaar had to make was the result of a mistake by our own Steve Nicol. When teams are forced to defend under pressure – as Blackburn had to – the mental and physical demands can lead to tiredness and a lack of concentration. This inevitably takes its toll, and if the team exerting the pressure can capitalize on forced errors they have earned a just reward.

Thursday, 8 October: The televised breakfast-time draw for the third round of the Littlewoods Cup produced a tie that delighted the country at large but left Merseyside disappointed – Liverpool v Everton. I know the two sets of fans on Merseyside would prefer a game like this to be saved for the final at Wembley, where the two teams and their supporters have distinguished themselves on previous occasions in the FA Cup, Milk Cup and Charity Shield. It is not to be, however; and all the other teams in the competition will be very relieved to know that one of us, one of the favourites, has to go out.

Two things are certain. There will be a full house at Anfield when the game is played later this month and there will be an abundance of that special derby atmosphere unique to Merseyside. It is quite different from anything I have ever experienced – and I was weaned on the Rangers v Celtic rivalry in Glasgow. The record of the two Mersey clubs and their followers in derby matches is exemplary, and it is something we must earnestly wish will remain so.

Within hours of the draw being made both clubs launched plans to transmit the match from Anfield by closed-circuit TV on to a giant screen at Goodison Park, three-quarters of a mile away, thus giving some of the fans who will not be able to get match tickets a chance to see the whole game live.

Saturday, 10 October: Third Division Preston contacted us yesterday to ask if they could have our reserve midfielder Brian Mooney on loan. It would be good for Brian to get League experience and he agreed to go to Deepdale with the possibility of making the move permanent if all parties agree.

We woke up this morning at our hotel base for our scheduled League match at Wimbledon to the gloomy sight of rain, rain and more rain. The Plough Lane pitch was flooded in the deluge and the game was called off. Postponements have become familiar to us this season; again, we simply have to accept the situation and find a new date. The frustrating thing was making the return journey for nothing; but it was unavoidable.

Before our next match – a week today at home to First Division leaders QPR – several of our players will be away on international duty for their various countries in midweek. When you have players scattered all over Europe you just have to hope they report back injury-free and mentally sharp.

Thursday, 15 October: Peter Robinson informed me that Oxford United have been in touch regarding a transfer inquiry we had made about Ray Houghton, whose future has been the subject of media speculation for some time. From our first approach to Oxford I was confident that Ray would want to join us as long as the clubs could reach agreement. Now we have had the message that he can leave for an agreed fee of £800,000.

It was arranged that Ray would travel up to meet us on Saturday night after playing for Oxford in their home game with West Ham. This is great news for us – but it is not news that we can divulge. In the first place, the transfer has not yet been concluded and, second, we have to be bound by the stipulation from Oxford that the story will be released exclusively in the *Daily Mirror* because of Robert Maxwell's connection with the club whose chairman is his son Kevin.

We had a similar binding agreement with Oxford when we signed John Aldridge last season, and it meant real cloak and dagger stuff with the rest of the newspapers, radio and television. This is not something you would normally choose to do. However, if you want to sign a player and the selling club make a transfer conditional on certain terms, you have to go along with it – or miss out on the player. As somebody once said about politics, it is not what is perfect but what is possible.

Friday, 16 October: QPR manager Jim Smith's comments, reported in today's *Liverpool Daily Post*, demanded a stern, public answer. 'I will be very interested to see who the referee is,' Smith was quoted as saying about tomorrow's match. He went on: 'The crowd there is tremendous and they put a lot of pressure on officials. I think you would have to knock down both ends of the ground before a visiting team could even think of winning a penalty there.' The issue was raised at my Press conference at Anfield, giving me the ideal opportunity to counter Smith's claims. I told the Press that in my view people who say such things are the ones pressurizing referees. If people like Jim Smith are referring to the number of penalties we have been awarded – six so far this season, four at home and two away – then I would immediately argue that we have also seen a number of decisions go against us, that we should in fact have been awarded more than we have had.

The fact of the matter is that we attack probably more than any other team and, as a result, more tackles are made on our players in the opposition's penalty area. If defenders do not tackle properly in the box, a penalty should be given. The discipline of our players so far this season has been exemplary. Not a single first-team player has been booked for dissent, and our only caution for any offence was for a foul by Gary Gillespie on David Speedie at Coventry back in August. Just because our players do not make mass protests to referees about decisions does not mean they agree with them. It simply means that they respect officials. There have been penalties we should have had and did not get; and because our lads did not make a fuss and got on with the game, the media have ignored the justice of our case.

Thankfully, all our players away on international duty this week returned injury-free and I was able to name the side that had been selected for last week's postponed match at Wimbledon, with Paul Walsh and Mark Lawrenson as substitutes.

A familiar face was back at Anfield today. Ian Rush popped in for a cup of tea and to renew old acquaintances. He will be at tomorrow's match, so I hope we can put on a good show for our celebrated 'old boy'.

▶ *The pulling power of success. Queues of people snaking their way to Anfield for our League game against QPR.*

▼ *A famous face in the stand: Ian Rush took advantage of a weekend break from his Italian job with Juventus to watch us play QPR.*

Saturday, 17 October: It is deeply ironical that in the aftermath of Jim Smith's remarks we suffered an adverse refereeing decision in the 14th minute of the match against QPR. Craig Johnston put the ball in the net but referee Ron Bridges chalked it off and awarded, instead, a free kick for Kevin Brock's foul on Peter Beardsley. The decision incensed the crowd – judging by their reaction – and it certainly did not please our players. But, as they have done before this season, they used disappointment to spur them on and, appropriately, it was Craig who finally put us ahead four minutes before half-time – a lovely move that flowed from Barry Venison, to Ronnie Whelan and then John Aldridge sent John Barnes gliding past Warren Neill to supply the cross for Craig to score. Bruce Grobbelaar played his part in sending us in for the break 1-0 up against the current leaders; he made impressive saves from both Gary Bannister and Ian Dawes.

▼*John Barnes watches the first of his two goals hit the net.*

▼ *All in a tangle! QPR defender Warren Neill tries to contain John Barnes as John Aldridge prepares to take possession.*

Jim Smith and his side can have no complaints about the justice of the penalty that put us 2-0 up after 65 minutes. Dean Coney handled the ball after a John Barnes free kick, and John Aldridge struck from the spot to set a new club record of scoring in nine consecutive League games in the same season. John then contributed to our third goal, when a one-two sent Barnesie in to score after 77 minutes. And if that excited the crowd they were absolutely ecstatic seven minutes later with a magnificent piece of football from Barnesie. He made a great run from the halfway line, past a string of Rangers men, before smashing his second goal of the match into the Kop net to follow up his midweek double for England against Turkey.

This win has put us at the top of Division One, ahead of Rangers on goal difference, and we have two games in hand. But position does not matter at this stage. Points and per-formances count and our lads have again successfully negotiated a sweeper system designed to frustrate them – and they have done it in style.

Before meeting Ray Houghton this evening I called in at a Liverpool hotel. I had promised Alan Hansen to appear at one of his testimonial functions. My wife Marina and I spent an enjoyable time there before leaving and driving to the Southport restaurant where Peter Robinson, chairman John Smith and I had arranged to meet Ray and his wife.

We reached agreement with Ray very quickly. He was very keen to join us – and link up again with his former team-mate John Aldridge – and he will have a medical and sign in the morning. He will then accompany us on our trip to Scotland for George McGeachie's testimonial match at Dundee. But everything must be kept secret under the terms of the transfer agreement with Oxford.

LIVERPOOL	QUEENS PARK RANGERS

First Division	Anfield
17 October	43,735

LIVERPOOL 4 (Johnston, Aldridge pen, Barnes 2)

QPR 0

LIVERPOOL	QPR
Grobbelaar	Seaman
Gillespie	Neill
Venison	Dawes
Nicol	Parker
Whelan	McDonald
Hansen	Fenwick
Beardsley	Allen
Aldridge	Coney
Johnston	Bannister
Barnes	Byrne
McMahon	Brock
SUBSTITUTES:	
Walsh	Pizanti
Lawrenson	Maguire

◀ *QPR players protest to referee Ron Bridges after his decision to award us a penalty. But he remained unmoved, and John Aldridge scored our second goal of the match when the referee ordered the kick to be taken.*

Sunday, 18 October: Ray passed his medical at Anfield and he has been given clearance to play for us at Dundee tomorrow night. But our big secret has leaked out. Some supporters who were queuing at Anfield for match tickets saw and recognized Ray; they immediately telephoned local radio stations and newspapers.

We arrived at the hotel in Scotland to find numerous telephone messages that had been left for me by journalists and radio people. But I still could not talk to them about Ray Houghton; my obligation is to wait until news of the transfer has been published in the first editions of the *Daily Mirror* later tonight.

However, no matter how careful you are it is always possible to make a slip in situations like this and, unwittingly, I did. A local Dundee photographer arrived at the hotel and asked to take a group picture of the players before their evening meal. I gave him permission to do so, forgetting that Ray would be in the photograph. It was a totally innocent mistake on my part but there was nothing I could do about it. The picture is to be published tomorrow to help boost George McGeachie's testimonial, and Ray is sure to be recognized. Nevertheless, the secret will be public knowledge tonight after the *Mirror*'s first editions have hit the streets. So fortunately the embargo will have held despite my faux pas!

I believe that Ray will prove a sound acquisition for us. Journalists will undoubtedly ask why I wanted to sign another midfield player when we already have a powerful contingent of players in that position. When answering this kind of question my reply is always that our aim is not just to have a good team but a good squad. We like to improve it whenever we can and since becoming manager I have endeavoured to keep our pool of talent topped up, because this has been Liverpool's trademark for many years. And there is no doubt that signing Ray Houghton is part of this process. I have admired his play for some time now and Oxford were made aware of our interest. Ray loves football – which is a good basis – and he has vision, good passing ability, he is quick and he always gives one hundred per cent. In addition to these qualities, he can play right across midfield from left to right, so he has a lot going for him.

The media, I'm sure, will not be slow to point out the financial aspect of this latest transfer, that since I became manager we have signed nine players for a total of almost £5.5 million. However, my chief responsibility as manager is to try to ensure, to the best of my ability and means, the uniquely high playing standards of Liverpool Football Club in English foot-

▼ *Ray Houghton in the thick of the action on his Liverpool senior debut.*

ball, which means having a squad of quality and quantity. I would be failing in my job if I did not approach it in that way. If I was frightened to back my judgment and that of our scouting staff because of the size of the fee required for a player, I would not be carrying out my duties.

The fact is that any money the club has for new players, for squad strengthening, is there to be used. The policy of chairman John Smith, the board and our chief executive Peter Robinson is that Liverpool FC is not in the business of hoarding huge profits from income provided by our loyal supporters. It is the club's belief that whenever necessary and possible this money should be ploughed back into reinforcing our major asset – the playing staff. It is called reinvestment.

The fans, whose wonderful support gives us so much encouragement, have a right to expect that we will use the money they spend in the best possible way. Of course, a lot has been spent on spectator facilities and other Anfield improvements but the team on the field remains our No.1 priority.

Monday, 19 October: It is ideal that we signed Ray in time for him to make the trip with us to Dundee. It will have helped him settle in and get to know the rest of the lads, while the match itself was the perfect moment for him to pull on a Liverpool shirt for the first time. I decided to give Ray a starting place on the left of midfield, with John Barnes pushed up front to partner Peter Beardsley and John Aldridge rested.

After Barnes had put us 1-0 up in the first half, Ray had the satisfaction of marking his debut by scoring our second goal after an hour with a header. And two late goals by Ronnie Whelan and Barnesie gave us a 4-0 win – and I also managed to get in 45 minutes of action after going on as substitute for Peter Beardsley at half-time.

The attendance figure of 20,000 made it a successful testimonial game for George McGeachie.

Thursday, 22 October: We have made another important signing today: Ronnie Whelan has put pen to paper to sign a new four-year contract with us. I don't know who is happier about it – us or Dusty. He is a fine player of great ability and versatility; his qualities have been tested at the highest level and he has never been found wanting. So we are delighted that he has accepted a new contract. I think Ronnie will be very pleased, too. After coming to us from Dublin as a lad, he has grown up at Anfield and is still only twenty-six. The club is as much a part of him as he is a part of the club, and we can look forward to many more happy years together.

DUNDEE 0	
LIVERPOOL 4 (Barnes 2, Houghton, Whelan)	
George McGeachie Testimonial	**19 October**
LIVERPOOL	
Grobbelaar	SUBSTITUTES:
Gillespie	Dalglish
Venison	Hansen
Nicol	McMahon
Whelan	
Lawrenson	
Beardsley	
Spackman	
Johnston	
Barnes	
Houghton	

▲ *Barry Venison is challenged by Luton's Brian Stein.*

LUTON TOWN	LIVERPOOL
First Division	Kenilworth Road
24 October	12,452

LUTON 0

LIVERPOOL 1 (Gillespie)

LUTON	LIVERPOOL
Sealey	Grobbelaar
Breacker	Gillespie
Grimes	Venison
McDonough	Nicol
Foster	Whelan
Donaghy	Hansen
Wilson	Beardsley
B. Stein	Aldridge
Harford	Houghton
Allinson	Barnes
Weir	McMahon
SUBSTITUTES:	
M. Stein	Spackman
Johnson	Lawrenson

Saturday, 24 October: My decision to select Ray Houghton on the right of midfield for today's League game at Luton meant that Craig Johnston was the unfortunate player to lose his place. I can understand and sympathize with how he must have felt. Everyone wants to play. Every player wants to be in the team but, sadly, we can pick only eleven of them to be out there on the field. In any case, Ray cannot play in our next game – the Littlewoods Cup tie against Everton – because he is ineligible after appearing in the competition for Oxford. Therefore Craig has a chance of coming straight back.

But my main concern today was our match at Luton, for which Nigel Spackman and Mark Lawrenson were the substitutes. I have often voiced my dislike of Luton's plastic pitch and all other artificial surfaces. My view is that an artificial pitch can produce artificial football and I have yet to meet a player who is happy about them. When I repeated this last season – after losing 4-1 at Luton in the League and 3-0 in an FA Cup second replay – I was accused of sour grapes, of looking for excuses. In fact, I prefaced all my comments then by saying that Luton had deserved to win and that I was merely stating my opinion about artificial surfaces. That opinion has never changed, win, lose or draw.

Today's visit to Kenilworth Road proved a happy one for us: Gary Gillespie got the only goal of the game after 71 minutes to bring us three points and become our ninth player to score this season. Mick Harford crashed a header against our bar in the dying seconds but, overall, we deserved our victory. The fact that our goals are continuing to be spread amongst the team is extremely pleasing, as is the fact that Gary has claimed his first of the season – a great header from a Barnes corner.

I would like to say thanks to my old boss and predecessor Joe Fagan who made Gary his first signing from Coventry in the summer of 1983. Side by side with Gary's development as a Liverpool player of class and composure at the back has been his international success for Scotland. This underlines my belief that the best way a player can fulfil any international ambitions is to perform to the best of his ability for his club.

Wednesday, 28 October: The match Merseyside had been bracing itself for – Liverpool v Everton in the third round of the Littlewoods Cup at Anfield. As well as Craig Johnston's return to the team in place of cup-tied Ray Houghton, we had to make a change at right-back. Barry Venison's Achilles damage suffered at Luton – highlighting the injury risk on plastic pitches – was more serious than we thought and Mark Lawrenson took over from him.

▲ *Plastic explosive – Gary Gillespie, who headed the only goal of the game to give us victory on Luton's artificial surface.*

▶ *An Ireland v Scotland tussle during the Littlewoods Cup derby as Ronnie Whelan moves in to challenge Everton's Graeme Sharp.*

DIVISION ONE

		Home					Away				
	P	W	D	L	F	A	W	D	L	F	A	Pts
Arsenal	13	5	0	1	15	3	4	2	1	8	4	29
QPR	13	5	1	0	11	3	4	1	2	8	8	29
Liverpool	**10**	**5**	**0**	**0**	**17**	**2**	**4**	**1**	**0**	**12**	**4**	**28**
Nottm For	13	3	2	1	10	4	5	1	1	14	7	27
Man Utd	14	4	3	0	12	6	2	4	1	12	9	25
Chelsea	14	6	1	0	15	7	2	0	5	9	14	25
Everton	13	5	1	1	14	4	1	3	2	7	5	22
Tottenham ...	14	5	0	2	12	7	1	2	4	4	9	20
Southmptn ..	13	2	2	2	7	8	2	3	2	12	12	17
Oxford	13	4	0	2	14	10	1	2	4	4	11	17
Derby	13	2	2	3	5	5	2	2	2	6	9	16
Coventry	13	2	1	4	7	14	3	0	3	7	7	16
Wimbledon ..	12	1	3	1	8	6	3	0	4	7	9	15
West Ham	13	1	4	2	6	8	2	2	2	8	8	15
Newcastle	12	1	1	4	5	10	2	3	1	10	9	13
Portsmth	13	3	2	2	11	11	0	2	4	3	16	13
Luton	13	2	3	2	8	7	1	0	5	6	12	12
Sheff Wed	14	2	1	4	8	12	1	2	4	6	15	12
Norwich	14	2	2	3	8	9	1	0	6	2	10	11
Watford	12	1	2	3	3	7	1	0	5	3	9	8
Charlton	13	1	1	5	4	11	0	2	4	6	13	6

▲ *My opposite number on Merseyside, Colin Harvey, looks anxious during our Littlewoods Cup tie at Anfield. But he was smiling at the end – his Everton team won!*

The game was played at the usual, frantic derby pace and the atmosphere reached boiling-point. But the spirit of the contest was a tribute to every single player and was symbolized by one marvellous moment, when Steve McMahon and Peter Reid fiercely contested possession and then helped each other get to their feet. There was one hundred per cent commitment from everyone on the field, as well as hard tackles and no quarter given when the ball was there to be won. The behaviour of the teams, however, was exemplary and another great advertisement for the quality of Merseyside football.

It turned out to be a difficult contest for both sides, and one of very few chances. The two best opportunities fell to Everton's Graeme Sharp, but he failed to accept them and the tie seemed destined for a Goodison replay. However, fate went against us, and in favour of Everton, six minutes from the end. There did not seem to be much danger when Gary Stevens took a pot-shot from twenty-five yards; but the ball struck Gary Gillespie's heel and rolled into the Kop net with Bruce Grobbelaar beaten by the deflection and unable to do anything about it.

Naturally, we were disappointed to lose our first game of the season and to go out of the competition. But the best of luck to Everton in the rounds to come. That chapter is over now and we have to look forward to next Sunday and the live televised League game . . . against Everton.

LIVERPOOL	EVERTON
Littlewoods Cup	Anfield
28 October	44,071

LIVERPOOL 0

EVERTON 1 (Stevens)

LIVERPOOL	EVERTON
Grobbelaar	Southall
Gillespie	Stevens
Lawrenson	Van Den Hauwe
Nicol	Ratcliffe
Whelan	Watson
Hansen	Reid
Beardsley	Steven
Aldridge	Heath
Johnston	Sharp
Barnes	Snodin
McMahon	Wilson

SUBSTITUTES:
Walsh	Harper
Spackman	Clarke

NOVEMBER

Sunday, 1 November, 1987: I have learned something today about the present Liverpool team that I have not had the chance of knowing until now, something very encouraging – they simply hate the taste of defeat. Even though we lost last Wednesday's Littlewoods Cup game against Everton in rather unfortunate circumstances – to a late, deflected goal – our players came out today stung by that setback and produced another fine performance to beat Everton 2-0 in the League game, screened live by the BBC from Anfield.

Losing a game was something our players had not experienced since the opening pre-season game at Bayern Munich way back in July, and that was against opposition who already had several games under their belt whereas it was our first

▼ *Our lads salute Steve McMahon (second from left) after his opening goal in the victory over Everton at Anfield.*

▲ *An ecstatic Bruce Grobbelaar celebrates our second goal against Everton scored by Peter Beardsley in the 2-0 League win at Anfield.*

▶ *The joy of the Kop as personified by the self-titled 'Dr Fun' during the League derby match.*

LIVERPOOL	EVERTON

First Division	Anfield
1 November	44,760

LIVERPOOL 2 (McMahon, Beardsley)

EVERTON 0

LIVERPOOL	EVERTON
Grobbelaar	Southall
Gillespie	Stevens
Lawrenson	Van Den Hauwe
Nicol	Ratcliffe
Whelan	Watson
Hansen	Reid
Beardsley	Steven
Aldridge	Clarke
Johnston	Sharp
Barnes	Snodin
McMahon	Wilson

SUBSTITUTES:

Houghton	Mountfield
Molby	Harper

one. The team's response to the Littlewoods disappointment has been magnificent. The game was very similar to last week's match: sternly but fairly fought, absolute commitment, a tremendous atmosphere with the good behaviour of the supporters crowning another glittering promotion for Merseyside football.

Once again, there was not much between the two sides. Everton got the crucial break last Wednesday and today we won by scoring two superbly created and executed goals. John Barnes had the Kop – and I'm sure millions around the country – drooling when he struck a 35th-minute pass with the outside of his left foot for Steve McMahon to put us ahead. The same two players were involved in our second goal in the 70th minute. A cute back-heel from Barnesie gave Steve the chance to cross the ball and Peter Beardsley finished well.

It was a great result and an impressive performance by an essentially unchanged team; the only difference was that Mark Lawrenson switched to left-back and Steve Nicol to right-back, with Jan Molby, troubled by injuries since the summer, included in the thirteen as a substitute for the first time this season. The win took us back to the top of the table above Arsenal, who won at Newcastle yesterday.

Tuesday, 3 November: Congratulations to Craig Johnston on being called up as an addition to the England squad for the decisive European Championship qualifier in Yugoslavia next week. Bobby Robson has obviously been sufficiently impressed with Craig, and his call-up underlines once more my belief that if you perform well for your club it is the best – and only – way to enhance any international ambitions you may nurture.

Wednesday, 4 November: I kept the same team – with Ray Houghton and Jan Molby again the substitutes – for our 1-1 draw at Wimbledon. Considering the number of opportunities we created but failed to accept, it is disappointing that we did not collect all three points, even though the one we did get sent us back to the top of the table following Arsenal's win over Chelsea last night. The statisticians tell me that our draw has ensured the best-ever start to a League season in the club's history, our ten wins and two draws surpassing the opening results in 1961 and 1978.

However, when you create sufficient chances for victory and then end up drawing, it has to be regretted. We put Wimbledon under all sorts of pressure and should have had more than our single goal scored by Ray Houghton in his first move after replacing Craig Johnston in the 61st minute. We paid the price for not accepting more of our chances when Wimbledon forced an equalizer through Carlton Fairweather 11 minutes from the end. One thing you can rely on with Wimbledon is that they will never stop battling. They will always aim for the maximum from their efforts and make it difficult for you.

WIMBLEDON	LIVERPOOL
First Division	**Plough Lane**
4 November	**13, 454**

WIMBLEDON 1 (Fairweather)
LIVERPOOL 1 (Houghton)

WIMBLEDON	LIVERPOOL
Beasant	Grobbelaar
Ryan	Gillespie
Bedford	Lawrenson
Goodyear	Nicol
Gayle	Whelan
Thorn	Hansen
Fairweather	Beardsley
Gibson	Aldridge
Fashanu	Johnston
Sanchez	Barnes
Gannon	McMahon

SUBSTITUTES:	
Cork	Houghton
Hazel	Molby

◀ *Our goalscorer Ray Houghton challenges Wimbledon's John Gannon during the 1-1 draw at Plough Lane.*

Their direct physical style has earned them a barrage of criticism, just as Watford's did when they won promotion to the First Division. But you won't find me jumping on that bandwagon. They deserved their win in the League against us at Anfield last season, when they also knocked Everton out of the FA Cup. The way they want to play the game is their concern, not mine. My only concern about Wimbledon is how we play against them. And as they finished sixth in the First Division last season they have clearly been too much for many of their opponents to contend with.

Saturday, 7 November: With our scheduled home League game against Nottingham Forest postponed because of England's game in Belgrade next Wednesday, I went to Goodison Park to watch our Central League team beat Everton reserves 3-1. The match was watched by a crowd of 4207, bigger than today's attendance at the Second Division game between Shrewsbury and Blackburn and higher than many at today's first-round FA Cup ties.

However, our win was overshadowed by an ankle injury suffered by Jan Molby, who had put us ahead in the 27th minute, with our other goals coming in the second half from Mike Marsh and John Jeffers. It is another blow in a very unfortunate season for Jan, who broke his foot in pre-season training the day before we flew out for our summer tour of West Germany and Scandinavia in July. He was carried off in the 65th minute of the reserve match just as he was in contention again at first-team level, filling a substitute role in our last two League games against Everton and Wimbledon.

Thursday, 12 November: Steve Staunton, a midfielder we signed as a seventeen-year-old from Dundalk in 1986, today joined Bradford City on a month's loan. It will undoubtedly broaden his experience to play for a club involved in the Second Division promotion battle. Steve's loan move follows the completion earlier this week of Brian Mooney's £25,000 transfer to Preston. Brian, another Irish lad who joined us as a teenager, went to Deepdale on loan last month, and both he and Preston were keen to make it permanent. It will give Brian a much better chance of enjoying first-team football, which did not come his way at Anfield, and it goes without saying that we wish him every success.

These moves for Steve and Brian have come as Joe Ashton, Labour M.P. for Bassetlaw, persuaded thirty Commons Members to table a motion demanding a handicapping system for top clubs. He wants to see us and other big clubs have points deducted for what he calls 'excessive expenditure', and he has complained that we have internationals playing in the reserves or on the substitute's bench. In his *People* newspaper column, he reacted to criticism of his proposal by writing: 'Liverpool and Kenny Dalglish never bring on good young lads of their own like Ipswich or Leeds did. They are simply cheque-book champions as in Italy or Spain.

'Liverpool and Everton should carry a six-point handicap unless they off-load. Personally, I can't see why the Scousers get so angry. When their city is bottom of the league for jobs they don't hesitate to ask for a hand-out.'

Quite apart from being totally unworkable – would a club, for instance, be penalized for playing an international in the reserves as part of his fitness programme following injury? – the whole idea is ridiculous. Liverpool FC have enjoyed a quarter of a century of success because they have always sought the best, both in players and performance. This pursuit has demanded money to build – and add to – the squad that is essential in the chase for honours. Without money it would not have been possible. The funds provided by our supporters have enabled the club to maintain its policy of pursuing excellence; and the only place into which money has been pumped is the red jerseys.

As for the accusation that we do not develop youngsters here, Joe Ashton is way off beam. Our playing standards at Anfield are sky-high and they have to be to keep us in a challenging position. It does not give us any pleasure, however, to have to tell a kid that we do not feel he will have a future with us. It is just a sad but necessary part of managing and coaching at our level. But just because few youngsters come through the ranks and into our first team does not mean we are not contributing to their development. Quite the opposite, in fact. A series of young players who have not made it with us have gone on to carve out successful careers for themselves in League football at some level and both they and their clubs are grateful for the grounding they had during their formative years with us.

Joe Ashton also referred in not very complimentary terms to Merseyside's unemployment problem. Politics is not my business and I have no wish to be involved in it. But both Liverpool and Everton have a right to be proud of what they have done for the city. The area is a jobs blackspot and both clubs have given the public some bright and welcome relief from the gloom that envelops many people's lives on Merseyside. I would have thought that was abundantly clear to someone like Joe Ashton.

▼ *Joe Ashton, the Labour M.P. whose proposal to handicap successful clubs is one with which I totally disagree.*

◀ *Bruce Grobbelaar gathers the ball under pressure from Bryan Robson.*

▼ *Ronnie Moran and me on our feet in the Old Trafford dug-out during the 1-1 draw with Manchester United.*

MANCHESTER UNITED	LIVERPOOL

First Division	Old Trafford
15 November	47,106

MAN UNITED 1 (Whiteside)

LIVERPOOL 1 (Aldridge)

MAN UNITED	LIVERPOOL
Walsh	Grobbelaar
Anderson	Gillespie
Gibson	Lawrenson
Duxbury	Nicol
Blackmore	Whelan
Moran	Hansen
Robson	Beardsley
Strachan	Aldridge
McClair	Johnston
Whiteside	Barnes
Olsen	McMahon
SUBSTITUTES:	
O'Brien	Houghton
Davenport	Spackman

Sunday, 15 November: Our internationals who were on midweek European Championship duty for England and Scotland returned free from injury to line up in an unchanged side for our game at Manchester United – another live TV match screened this time by ITV.

The previews of the match quoted the statistics that Liverpool had won only one and lost seven of the previous fifteen League meetings between the clubs, and even claimed that United have a jinx on us. That is ridiculous. I don't go along with talk of hoodoos or such like. In the games they have beaten us, United have been better than us on the day, no more, no less. But I am sure they would swap places with us after all the success this club has had while United have not fulfilled the standards people came to expect from a club of their stature. The reasons for that are not my business. They are the concern of those employed by Manchester United.

We went ahead today with a superb move after 20 minutes: a fine pass from Alan Hansen found Steve McMahon, whose cross was headed in by John Aldridge for his thirteenth goal of the season. The game was the usual hard-fought battle we had anticipated, and United's equalizer was an outrageous misfortune for us: referee David Scott failed to spot Kevin Moran's hand-ball offence before Norman Whiteside put the ball in the net. Viewers around the country saw how blatant it was on the TV playbacks, but the fact that our players did not make a song-and-dance about it underlines their respect for officials and shows why we have not had a single caution for dissent this season. In fact, Steve McMahon's booking today for a foul on Bryan Robson was only our second of the campaign so far.

While the circumstances of United's equalizer were so rough on us – as was a rejected penalty claim when Aldridge was brought down in the box – I think a draw was a fair result overall. Such are our standards that when we get a point away from home it is considered that we have dropped two points. But United dropped two at home today.

Saturday, 21 November: Norwich today became the first team to prevent us scoring in the First Division this season by holding us to a goalless draw at Anfield. And all credit to them. They played well and their Scottish goalkeeper Bryan Gunn had a tremendous game on his first Anfield appearance, producing some magnificent saves.

While Norwich rightly will be pleased with their performance – they came to contain us and did it well – we contributed to our own downfall by failing to take chances, quite apart from those opportunities denied us by Gunn. It was up to us to

◄ *Aldridge takes the applause after heading us in front.*

◀ Norwich defender Steve Bruce gets in a clearance under pressure from Peter Beardsley.

LIVERPOOL	NORWICH CITY
First Division	Anfield
21 November	37,446
LIVERPOOL 0	
NORWICH 0	
LIVERPOOL	NORWICH
Grobbelaar	Gunn
Gillespie	Brown
Lawrenson	Elliott
Nicol	Bruce
Whelan	Phelan
Hansen	Butterworth
Beardsley	Crook
Aldridge	Drinkell
Houghton	Rosario
Barnes	Putney
McMahon	Gordon
SUBSTITUTES:	
Johnston	Biggins
Spackman	Goss

try to break down Norwich and we failed to do it. Our first League blank – our only other goalless outing so far was the Littlewoods Cup defeat by Everton – coincided with Ray Houghton's home debut. But Ray, taking over on the right of midfield from Craig Johnston, who was switched to substitute, showed what a fine player and passer he is and helped us create a bundle of chances that went begging.

We sent on Craig in place of Peter Beardsley after 64 minutes just to try something different and to see if it would prise Norwich open. Craig went to the right flank and Ray moved to the left, allowing John Barnes to operate in a central role.

However, we just could not get that elusive goal and Norwich were delighted to end a run of eight consecutive defeats on Merseyside in the various competitions with a display that earned them the Barclays Performance of the Week Award, even though Southampton won 1-0 at Highbury against League leaders Arsenal.

Tuesday, 24 November: We recaptured our goal touch tonight and went back to the top of the First Division – and the result was worth the wait. At half-time against Watford it was 0-0, and we had a few scares about conceding one ourselves in the first half. After the interval, though, it was a totally

▶ Before the curtain goes up. Some scenes in our dressing-room before our 4-0 win over Watford: John Barnes and I deep in conversation; Ronnie Moran jokes with Peter Beardsley, while massaging Alan Hansen; a good-luck message for John Aldridge from John Barnes as the lads prepare to take the field.

LIVERPOOL	WATFORD
First Division	Anfield
24 November	32,396

LIVERPOOL 4 (McMahon, Houghton, Aldridge, Barnes)

WATFORD 0

LIVERPOOL	WATFORD
Grobbelaar	Coton
Gillespie	Chivers
Lawrenson	Jackett
Nicol	Sherwood
Whelan	Morris
Hansen	McClelland
Beardsley	Blissett
Aldridge	Allen
Houghton	Senior
Barnes	Porter
McMahon	Hodges

SUBSTITUTES:	
Walsh	Rostron
Spackman	Sterling

different story, with John Barnes seizing the starring role against his former club, watched by England manager Bobby Robson.

Within ten minutes of the re-start Barnesie had helped to break the deadlock when his perfectly-timed pass caught out his former team-mates and gave Steve McMahon the opportunity to loft a shot into the Kop net as goalkeeper Tony Coton raced off his line. Nine minutes later Ray Houghton made it 2-0 when he beat John McClelland to the ball and scored with a shot that deflected off Kenny Jackett and looped over Coton into the net. It was 3-0 in the 68th minute when a great cross from Barnesie gave John Aldridge the chance to head his fourteenth goal of the season. Barnes the creator became Barnes the executor in the 72nd minute when he scored a beauty, playing a one-two with Steve McMahon before sending a twenty-five-yard scorcher past Coton and into the net – a great strike.

So in contrast to Norwich last Saturday, there was no satisfaction for Watford who have still to win a First Division point on Merseyside. But it was a very satisfying night for us.

Saturday, 28 November: The hype for today's game at Tottenham had been building up all last week because it was the first match with Terry Venables in charge of the team following his appointment as their new manager. Our team bus was delayed in traffic en route to the ground, so my team talk in the White Hart Lane dressing-room was a little later than planned. But none of these problems spilled over on to the pitch and we won 2-0.

Tottenham had been without a manager for six games between David Pleat's departure and Terry's arrival from Barcelona. He had not made any forecasts about today's game but the media were full of advance publicity, pointing out that in his previous spells as a manager in England at Crystal Palace and QPR his teams had never beaten or even scored a goal against Liverpool in five attempts. Today made it number six. All I can say is that now Terry is back in this country he will have more opportunities to try to beat us in the future.

I believe Tottenham must take credit for bringing him back from abroad and obviously he will instil some of his own personality into the side because every manager has his own ideas and views. Terry was at Tottenham only a week before the game against us, and in the opening 20 minutes today his side was reduced to ten men when midfielder Steve Hodge was sent off for fouling Ray Houghton.

We had to go into the game without Peter Beardsley, whose knee injury meant that Paul Walsh started his first senior match of the season. Both our goals came from lay-offs by John

TOTTENHAM HOTSPUR	LIVERPOOL

First Division	White Hart Lane
28 November	47,362

TOTTENHAM 0

LIVERPOOL 2 (McMahon, Johnston)

TOTTENHAM	LIVERPOOL
Parks	Grobbelaar
Hughton	Gillespie
Thomas	Lawrenson
Ruddock	Nicol
Fairclough	Whelan
Mabbutt	Hansen
C. Allen	Walsh
P. Allen	Aldridge
Waddle	Houghton
Hodge	Barnes
Stevens	McMahon
SUBSTITUTES:	
Claesen	Spackman
O'Shea	Johnston

◀ *John Barnes places the ball for a corner during our victory over Tottenham.*

▶ *A striking action shot of John Barnes during our 2-0 win at White Hart Lane.*

▶ *Craig Johnston celebrates scoring our second goal after going on as a substitute.*

DIVISION ONE

	P	W	D	L	F	A	W	D	L	F	A	Pts
		Home					**Away**					
Liverpool	**16**	**7**	**1**	**0**	**23**	**2**	**5**	**3**	**0**	**16**	**6**	**40**
Arsenal	17	6	0	2	18	5	5	2	2	12	8	35
QPR	17	5	3	0	12	4	4	2	3	10	12	32
Nottm For	15	4	2	1	15	4	5	1	2	16	10	30
Everton	17	6	2	1	17	5	2	3	3	8	7	29
Man Utd	16	4	4	0	13	7	2	4	2	13	11	26
Chelsea	17	6	2	0	16	8	2	0	7	10	19	26
Wimbledon ..	17	3	4	1	13	8	3	2	4	11	13	24
Southmptn ..	17	3	2	3	11	10	3	3	3	13	14	23
Derby	16	3	2	3	7	5	3	3	2	8	10	23
Tottenham ...	18	5	1	3	13	10	1	3	5	4	11	22
Oxford	17	5	1	2	16	11	1	3	5	4	14	22
Luton	16	4	3	2	14	7	2	0	5	8	12	21
West Ham	17	2	4	3	9	11	2	3	3	9	11	19
Coventry	17	2	3	4	10	17	3	1	4	9	10	19
Newcastle	16	2	2	4	7	11	2	4	2	11	14	18
Sheff Wed	17	3	1	5	11	15	2	2	4	7	15	18
Portsmth	17	3	3	3	11	12	1	2	5	4	21	17
Watford	17	3	2	3	7	8	1	2	6	4	14	16
Norwich	18	2	2	5	10	14	1	1	7	2	12	12
Charlton	17	2	2	5	8	13	0	2	6	8	17	10

Aldridge, highlighting the fact that he is a maker as well as a taker of opportunities. When he knocked the ball to Steve McMahon in the 63rd minute it gave Steve the chance to collect his fifth goal of the season. After replacing Paul Walsh two minutes after that goal, Craig Johnston proceeded to etch his name on the scoresheet by turning in John Aldridge's flick-on from Steve Nicol's cross eight minutes from the end.

We thoroughly deserved our victory and, in addition to the three points, it was very pleasing to have kept another clean sheet – the eighth in our last ten League outings.

Monday, 30 November: I was back at Parkhead tonight for Davie Provan's Testimonial match between Celtic and Nottingham Forest. Davie, sadly, had to quit football through illness and I was delighted to travel up to Glasgow to try to make some contribution to his testimonial fund.

I was called off the substitute's bench to join the action after 23 minutes, taking over from Paul McStay, and I made a major impact on Celtic's performance. The score when I went on was 1-1 – and we ended up losing 3-1! But that, of course, didn't matter. The important thing was that more than 42,000 people turned out on a freezing night to salute Davie, which is a great tribute to him and the attitude of the Glasgow public.

DECEMBER

LIVERPOOL	CHELSEA
First Division	**Anfield**
6 December	**31,211**

LIVERPOOL 2 (Aldridge pen, McMahon)

CHELSEA 1 (Durie pen)

LIVERPOOL	CHELSEA
Grobbelaar	Freestone
Gillespie	Clarke
Lawrenson	Dorigo
Nicol	Pates
Whelan	McLaughlin
Hansen	Wood
Beardsley	Nevin
Aldridge	Murphy
Houghton	Dixon
Barnes	Durie
McMahon	C. Wilson

SUBSTITUTES:	
Spackman	Hall
Johnston	K. Wilson

Sunday, 6 December, 1987: Another live televised Sunday afternoon game brought Chelsea to Anfield, where they had not won in the League for fifty-two years. But as I have always responded to statistics of this nature, the past counts for nothing. It's just history. Every game has to be won and our lads certainly had to battle to come out 2-1 winners today – a result that rewarded their commitment and sheer spirit as well as their skill.

We were a goal down after 21 minutes: Gordon Durie scored from the spot after referee George Courtney had awarded a penalty for Mark Lawrenson's challenge on Pat Nevin. It was Gordon's twenty-second birthday and no doubt he will long remember it for the kick he put past Bruce Grobbelaar into the roof of the Kop net for his thirteenth goal of the season. The onus is always on the home team and when you go a goal

▶ *John Barnes goes past Chelsea's grounded defender Joe McLaughlin.*

behind as we did then that onus is even more firmly placed on you. It was the first League goal we had conceded at home since Charlton in September. However, we went about the job in the right way; we kept playing football and we maintained the pressure.

Peter Beardsley, having recovered from the knee injury that kept him out of the side at Tottenham, returned in place of Paul Walsh, and Gary Gillespie and Steve Nicol were both fit enough to play after missing Scotland's midweek match in Luxemburg. Gary, in fact, went close to equalizing for us 10 minutes before the interval, but Clive Wilson was there to clear his header off the line. A string of other scoring attempts were denied us by some splendid goalkeeping from Roger Freestone.

We forced seven corners in the opening 13 minutes of the second half and John Barnes hit the post before we finally equalized in the 67th minute. John Aldridge was moving through the Chelsea penalty area when Joe McLaughlin clipped his heel and sent him crashing to the turf. Aldridge got up and calmly tucked away his eighth spot kick from eight attempts this season, to increase his overall goal tally to fifteen.

Six minutes from the end we were still pressing forward, but the score remained at 1-1. We pulled off Aldridge and sent on Craig Johnston, releasing Barnes into a central striking role. We decided to do this simply to try to win the game; it was

▼ *John Aldridge goes sprawling after a challenge by Joe McLaughlin, for which referee George Courtney awarded a penalty. He got up and scored our equalizer from the spot, sending goalkeeper Roger Freestone the wrong way.*

no reflection whatever on the player substituted. It was just a case of utilizing our resources in a different way – and fortunately it paid dividends. With three minutes left, Barnesie's magnificent return pass sent Ray Houghton in on the left to cut the ball back for Steve McMahon to score the winner and complete three consecutive scoring appearances after his goals against Tottenham and Watford.

It was a magnificent game that was a credit to the players of both sides. The 31,000-plus crowd at Anfield and millions watching on television were treated to some gripping entertainment.

▼ *Our Central League team before the home reserve game against Nottingham Forest on 8 December, a match I am pictured watching from the dug-out with reserve team coach Phil Thompson and Ronnie Moran who, for a few seconds, apparently cannot bear to watch! And the Kop, deserted except for two ball-boys, provides a stark contrast to first-team match days.*

Monday, 7 December: Our chairman John Smith today
announced another 'signing' of crucial importance to Liverpool
FC – a new extension to his present contract for Peter Robinson,
our widely respected general secretary and chief executive.
The seven-and-a-half-year addition to his current agreement
spans the years until 1995, when Peter will have completed
thirty years with the club, and it is comforting to know that
the administrative affairs of Liverpool will be in such capable
hands for a good few years yet. As the chairman said: 'This
club has made many fine signings but when Peter joined
Liverpool from Brighton in 1965 it was one of the finest we
have made this century. He is the most professional of
administrators and the finest chief executive and general
secretary in Britain if not Europe.'

Saturday, 12 December: Disappointment is my overriding
reaction to our 2-2 draw at Southampton this afternoon. We
were 2-0 up through goals by John Barnes in the 11th and
38th minutes, yet we contrived to throw away that lead and
two points with it.

I will never reveal details of what the players, the backroom
staff and myself discuss in the dressing-room. That must
always remain private. However, my feelings after this game
were based on the need to underline that the only justifiable
reason for losing a lead like that is if it is achieved by the
opposition being so much better than you. But in this case we
had to examine our own game for the reasons. We had to look
at ourselves. Although we lost Mark Lawrenson with a hamstring injury after 19 minutes, with Gary Ablett replacing
him, it does not explain our slipshod second-half performance
which was in such contrast to our play before the interval.

Colin Clarke scored for Southampton just before half-time;
Andy Townsend hit their equalizer after 71 minutes and it
needed a goal-line clearance by Steve Nicol from a Matthew
Le Tissier header in the dying seconds not only to ensure that
we got a point but also to keep alive our unbeaten League run,
which has now stretched to eighteen games. We should not
have allowed that possibility to occur after playing so well
earlier in the game, which had been highlighted by Barnesie's
volleyed goal set up by John Aldridge and then his finish to a
six-man move to score our second goal from twenty yards.

Thursday, 17 December: Before I and members of our
coaching staff attended the annual Christmas lunch for the
Merseyside clubs given by representatives of the national
Press, we arranged for Kevin MacDonald to join his former

SOUTHMPTN	LIVERPOOL
First Division	**The Dell**
12 December	**19,507**

SOUTHMPTN 2 (Clarke, Townsend)

LIVERPOOL 2 (Barnes 2)

SOUTHMPTN	LIVERPOOL
Burridge	Grobbelaar
Forrest	Gillespie
Statham	Lawrenson
Case	Nicol
Moore	Whelan
Bond	Hansen
Townsend	Beardsley
Cockerill	Aldridge
Clarke	Houghton
Baker	Barnes
D. Wallace	McMahon
SUBSTITUTES:	
Le Tissier	Spackman
R. Wallace	Ablett

▶ *The outstretched boot of
airborne Southampton defender
Gerry Forrest clears the ball from
Steve McMahon, an incident that
led to our first goal which John
Barnes is seen firing past goalkeeper John Burridge.*

club Leicester on a month's loan.

Kevin has shown tremendous determination to regain fitness since he was carried off with a fractured left leg at Southampton back in September 1986. He has already made eight Central League appearances, and a month with Second Division Leicester can only help him in his comeback programme.

Saturday, 19 December: Although we lost one player through injury we had the good fortune to welcome back another after a lengthy absence. While Mark Lawrenson was ruled out of today's home game with Sheffield Wednesday because of the hamstring injury he suffered at Southampton last week, Barry Venison was fit to take over at right-back after being out for two months with an Achilles injury sustained on Luton's plastic pitch in October.

Today proved another test for the determination of our players to stick to their task of playing football in an attempt to break down stubborn opponents. They were rewarded with a 1-0 victory through Gary Gillespie's second goal of the season which was scored in the last quarter of an hour – and it clinched our team a place in the record books.

Wednesday, who had not lost in three previous Anfield visits since returning to the First Division, repeated last season's ploy of utilizing a man in front of their back four, this time giving Gary Megson the job. They made it difficult for us; but John Aldridge sent a header crashing against the bar before Martin Hodge tipped over Ronnie Whelan's header for the 76th-minute corner that brought our goal. John Barnes came in for some criticism for the corner he took, which was short. But there is a worse way to take one – by putting it into the crowd – and certainly this one paid off because Ray Houghton was alert enough to flick the ball on across goal for Gary to score with a shot that went in off a post.

It was Gary's second goal of the season and his second 'three-pointer' because he also scored the only goal of the game at Luton in October. Once again our winner came after we had made a substitution: Craig Johnston replaced Peter Beardsley for the last 20 minutes, allowing Barnesie to move into the middle. But we don't claim any divine inspiration for a change like that. As I have said before, you just try something to see if the change can produce that little break you need.

Our win, putting us seven points clear at the top, took our undefeated League sequence since the start of the season to nineteen games, equalling the club's best-ever First Division start set in 1949-50. The match also had a memorable off-beat moment when Wednesday, for a few seconds late in the game, actually had twelve men on the pitch. Colin West and Larry May were sent on as substitutes and only Gary Owen went off! But referee John Watson – with a little help from our dug-out – was alerted to the mix-up and Mark Chamberlain eventually went off as well. My opposite number Howard Wilkinson joked afterwards: 'I thought the old 4-4-4 formation would have done it – that was Plan B if we went a goal down!'

LIVERPOOL   SHEFFIELD WEDNESDAY

First Division	Anfield
19 December	35,383

LIVERPOOL 1 (Gillespie)
SHEFFIELD 0

LIVERPOOL	SHEFFIELD
Grobbelaar	Hodge
Gillespie	Sterland
Venison	Worthington
Nicol	Madden
Whelan	Pearson
Hansen	Proctor
Beardsley	Marwood
Aldridge	Owen
Houghton	Chapman
Barnes	Megson
McMahon	Chamberlain

SUBSTITUTES:

Johnston	West
Ablett	May

◀ *Sheffield Wednesday goal-keeper Martin Hodge just beats John Aldridge in a tussle for possession at Anfield.*

▼ *Ray Houghton moves in as Nigel Worthington attempts a clearance.*

We have now played every First Division team except Nottingham Forest, and still to be unbeaten reflects great credit on the players. I have read that the bookies have slashed the odds against us completing the League season undefeated to 14-1. This makes it neither more nor less possible, but if any team is going to achieve the feat it has to be us, because we are the only unbeaten side. The pleasing thing is that our run is not proving a burden to the players. We *are* just taking each match as it comes. That is easy to say but hard to do. However, it is, and always has been, our approach. Tomorrow, though, we can all let our hair down – or something like that – when the players have their regular fancy-dress Christmas party.

Sunday, 20 December: My name was briefly changed from 'boss' to 'My Lord' tonight because I went to our bash dressed as a judge, complete with wig and gown. It was so enjoyable that I sentenced them to hold another one next year!

Boxing Day, Saturday, 26 December: After a taste of Christmas with my family yesterday, I headed south with the team for today's game at Oxford which brought Ray Houghton and John Aldridge face-to-face with their former team-mates in an unchanged side. This was our twentieth League game of the season, bringing us to the halfway stage of the League programme, and our 3-0 win not only preserved our unbeaten run but also established a new slot in the Liverpool FC record books as our record start to a First Division season. Achievements like this are not in the same bracket as winning trophies – which are the only indisputable yardsticks of success – but the knowledge that they have contributed to something that no other Liverpool team in history has done is something in which the lads can take pleasure and satisfaction.

Our victory today, while Nottingham Forest were winning at Arsenal, has given us a ten-point lead at the top of the First Division and, in itself, that is very pleasing. We would rather be top than in any other position, but there is still half the season left to negotiate. Ray Houghton and John Aldridge were both involved in our opening goal against their old club. We had won sixteen of the seventeen corners in the first half but had to wait until three minutes before the interval before taking the lead. A cross from Ray gave Ronnie Whelan the chance of a header, which was blocked on the line by Oxford goalkeeper Peter Hucker, and John Aldridge pounced on the loose ball to put us ahead.

At the start of the second half, Oxford put us under a lot of pressure as they kicked down the sloping pitch towards their

OXFORD UNITED	LIVERPOOL

First Division	Manor Ground
26 December	13,680

OXFORD 0

LIVERPOOL 3 (Aldridge, Barnes, McMahon)

OXFORD	LIVERPOOL
Hucker	Grobbelaar
Bardsley	Gillespie
Dreyer	Venison
Shelton	Nicol
Hill	Whelan
Caton	Hansen
Hebberd	Beardsley
Whitehurst	Aldridge
Saunders	Houghton
Phillips	Barnes
Rhoades-Brown	McMahon

SUBSTITUTES:

Foyle	Johnston
Mustoe	Spackman

▶ *Ray Houghton, our midfield signing from Oxford, runs out of the tunnel at his former club, this time as a Liverpool player. It was a successful homecoming as we won 3-0.*

▼ *John Aldridge, also back at his former club, finds himself denied a scoring opportunity by Oxford goalkeeper Peter Hucker.*

bank of supporters, and Bruce Grobbelaar had to save headers from Billy Whitehurst and Dean Saunders. However, one of many fine touches today by Peter Beardsley provided the pass that sent John Barnes in for a shot that beat Hucker and put us two up after 54 minutes. And just seven minutes later Steve McMahon made it 3-0 in spectacular style with a shot from almost thirty yards. It was Steve's fourth goal in six games and if he wants to fulfil his ambition of an England place he is going the right way about it by performing impressively for

▶ *Roy Evans treats Gary Gillespie for a knock he received during our Christmas win over Newcastle at Anfield.*

▼ *John Aldridge gets up off the turf after being fouled for the penalty from which he scored our second goal in the 4-0 victory over Newcastle.*

us. But I don't expect Bobby Robson to interfere with my team selection and you won't find me interfering with his.

The only blot for Steve this afternoon was his booking for a foul on Richard Hill. But it was only our third caution of the season, which is astonishingly low when you think of the level the lads are playing at and the efforts other teams make when they play Liverpool. In fact, I have had more bookings in a season than the entire first-team squad have had so far, which speaks volumes for their attitude and conduct on the field.

Another very pleasing factor of the season so far is that not only are we pulling in bigger crowds at Anfield but seven of our ten away League games have attracted the highest attendances of the season to date at those grounds. And one of the others, at Manchester United in November, was screened live on television and still drew a crowd of more than 47,000!

Monday, 28 December:　The boom at the box office was evident again today when the visit of Newcastle United drew 44,637 spectators to Anfield. They saw a tremendous game and, although we won 4-0, Newcastle produced a much better performance than the scoreline might suggest. The appearance of Brazilian import Mirandinha and England prospect Paul Gascoigne in the Newcastle ranks probably helped swell the attendance because I have constantly maintained that ability will always attract the public. Both these players made impressive contributions to Newcastle's performance – one delightful Mirandinha chip in the second half producing an equally memorable save by Bruce Grobbelaar – but on the day our players were worthy of their win because of the sheer quality of the football they produced.

Steve McMahon extended his blistering scoring sequence by shooting us ahead from twenty yards after only five minutes. We then had to wait until the 49th minute before adding to our lead with a penalty, awarded by referee John Key for Glenn Roeder's challenge on John Aldridge, who scored from the spot. Newcastle were furious at the decision and the media raised it at the after-match Press conference. My reaction is to ask why so much comment is made whenever we get a penalty and so little on the many occasions we have penalties refused. This is where the good behaviour of our lads rebounds on them. If they made mass protests about decisions they would generate publicity. But because they accept the decisions of the referees – which is far from saying they agree with them – our case hardly warrants a mention in the Press or on radio and television. We have scored more goals than anyone else in the First Division, we put together more passes, we have more

◀ *Ronnie Whelan fires in a shot watched by Newcastle's grounded Paul Gascoigne.*

DIVISION ONE

	P	| Home					| Away					
	P	W	D	L	F	A	W	D	L	F	A	Pts
Liverpool	21	10	1	0	30	3	6	4	0	21	8	53
Nottm For	20	6	2	1	23	5	7	2	2	21	11	43
Arsenal	22	7	1	3	22	9	5	3	3	13	11	40
Man Utd	21	6	4	0	18	9	4	4	3	17	13	38
Everton	22	8	2	1	22	5	2	5	4	10	10	37
QPR	22	6	3	2	16	10	4	3	4	11	17	36
Wimbledon ..	22	5	5	1	18	10	4	2	5	13	15	34
Chelsea	22	6	4	0	18	10	2	1	9	13	26	29
Luton	21	5	4	3	18	11	3	0	6	9	14	28
Southmptn ..	21	4	3	3	15	13	3	4	4	16	18	28
Tottenham ...	22	6	1	4	15	12	2	3	6	7	14	28
Sheff Wed	22	5	1	5	14	16	3	2	6	11	20	27
West Ham	22	4	4	4	14	15	2	4	4	11	14	26
Newcastle	21	3	3	4	9	12	3	4	4	15	21	25
Derby	21	3	3	5	10	10	3	3	4	9	15	24
Coventry	21	2	4	4	10	17	4	2	5	12	15	24
Oxford	22	5	1	5	17	19	1	3	7	7	20	22
Norwich	22	3	2	5	13	14	3	1	8	6	15	21
Portsmth	22	3	5	4	13	15	1	3	6	6	24	20
Charlton	22	3	4	5	12	16	1	2	7	9	18	18
Watford	21	3	2	5	8	12	1	4	6	6	16	18

LIVERPOOL	NEWCASTLE UNITED

First Division	**Anfield**
28 December	**44,637**

LIVERPOOL 4 (McMahon, Aldridge 2 inc. 1 pen, Houghton)

NEWCASTLE 0

LIVERPOOL	NEWCASTLE
Grobbelaar	Kelly
Gillespie	McDonald
Venison	Wharton
Nicol	McCreery
Whelan	Anderson
Hansen	Roeder
Beardsley	D. Jackson
Aldridge	Gascoigne
Houghton	Goddard
Barnes	Mirandinha
McMahon	Cornwell

SUBSTITUTES:

Johnston	Bogie
Spackman	Craig

possession and we are in the opposition penalty box so much that we are bound to be on the receiving end of more tackles. Therefore the number of incidents in the box is obviously going to be greater.

The penalty awarded to us today was our ninth of the season. It was hard to judge the incident from my vantage point in the dug-out but I can think of others this season we should have had and didn't get. Fortunately, the furore over the penalty did not ruffle Aldridge. In his usual ice-cool manner he beat Gary Kelly from the spot to put us 2-0 up. John was also on the end of our third goal after 76 minutes, which clocked up our League half-century and stretched his personal tally to eighteen. It was a tremendous goal, the product of some superb first-time passing involving Gary Gillespie, John Barnes and Peter Beardsley with Aldridge applying the finish. Our fourth came two minutes from time after we had sent on Craig Johnston and Nigel Spackman in place of Ronnie Whelan and John Barnes. Craig linked with Ray Houghton, whose shot hit the back of the Kop net after striking Neil McDonald on the way.

The bookies have now cut the odds against us completing the First Division programme unbeaten to 10-1 and they are quoting 8-1 *on* us winning the title. But the only figures I am concerned about are the ones in the final League table.

JANUARY

A great way to start the year as Peter Beardsley scores our first goal of 1988 with the first of our four against Coventry. Visiting midfielder Lloyd McGrath is helpless to prevent the ball hitting the net.

Friday, 1 January, 1988: Our players, who deserve tremendous credit for their performances up to the turn of the year, opened 1988 in marvellous style with a 4-0 home win over Coventry.

I think it was our 4-1 win at Coventry in late August, our second League fixture, that made the pundits sit up and take notice of this Liverpool team. Our win at Arsenal on the season's opening day was a close game that could have gone either way. But when we went to Highfield Road and toppled the FA Cup holders, a team many fancied to be in contention for the championship, there was much praise of our players, especially the new lads John Barnes, Peter Beardsley and John Aldridge, whose Anfield career was only just starting even though he signed for us last season.

Today's home win over Coventry was even more emphatic because again we scored four times and kept a clean sheet, our fourth in a row. We fielded an unchanged team but lost Barry Venison early in the second half with a calf injury. Gary Ablett went on to fill the left-back berth, with Steve Nicol switching to the right, and it speaks volumes for the players that they carried on without a hiccup.

Peter Beardsley had put us ahead in the 23rd minute and we were still leading only 1-0, mainly due to some impressive saves by our former reserve goalkeeper Steve Ogrizovic, when Barry had to go off. However, in the 54th minute Steve Nicol linked with Peter Beardsley and sent in a short cross for John Aldridge to make it 2-0, with his nineteenth goal of the season.

We scored our third in the 76th minute when a short free kick from John Barnes allowed Peter Beardsley to provide the pass for Ray Houghton to crack in his second goal in successive games. Nigel Spackman, who went on for Steve McMahon for the last 10 minutes, set up our fourth goal. He headed back an attempted pass from Brian Kilcline and Peter Beardsley climaxed a brilliant performance by firing his second goal of the game past Ogrizovic.

Nottingham Forest's home defeat by Newcastle today ensured us a thirteen-point lead at the top of the First Division. But the most pleasing factor of the season is that our players are not relying on anyone else to help them. They are going out and earning points by the quality of their performance. Perhaps that is what Coventry manager John Sillett had in mind when he said after the game: 'I didn't think it possible but Liverpool are working harder than ever.'

LIVERPOOL	COVENTRY CITY

First Division   Anfield

1 January   38,790

LIVERPOOL 4 (Beardsley 2, Aldridge, Houghton)

COVENTRY 0

LIVERPOOL	COVENTRY
Grobbelaar	Ogrizovic
Gillespie	Borrows
Venison	Downs
Nicol	McGrath
Whelan	Kilcline
Hansen	Smith
Beardsley	Bennett
Aldridge	Phillips
Houghton	Regis
Barnes	Speedie
McMahon	Gynn
SUBSTITUTES:	
Ablett	Livingstone
Spackman	Rodger

Monday, 4 January: John Wark, who has been in demand all season by clubs at home and abroad, today took up the opportunity of returning to his former club Ipswich. John, who joined us in a £450,000 move from Portman Road in 1984, continued at Anfield the scoring exploits that have been a highlight of his career. It is a habit he has never lost, as emphasized by the fact that he has scored a total of 176 goals in 488 senior games. That is a very impressive strike rate for a midfield player; for Liverpool alone he has scored forty-two goals in 106 appearances, which is a ratio many strikers would be proud to have.

Despite having had misfortune with injuries during his period at Liverpool he has done tremendously well for us and his departure will deplete our squad. In that sense we are sad to see him go, but at thirty he had to think of his future which is why we have not stood in his way. Although John is a fellow Glaswegian, he has gone back to his football 'home' because, after coming down from Scotland, he started as an apprentice at Ipswich. I hope his wish for regular senior football is now realized, after making only two first-team appearances for us this season.

As John packed his bags to leave, our reserve midfielder or defender Steve Staunton returned a week early from his loan period at Bradford City to ensure that he would not be cup-tied should he be needed in the FA Cup.

Saturday, 9 January: As expected, our goalkeeper Bruce Grobbelaar had no chance of playing today after his training mishap on Thursday. He was attempting to clear the ball during a session at Melwood when Steve McMahon caught him on the calf, gashing his leg. The wound has now turned septic. News of his injury was something I did not want revealed publicly because, whilst I appreciate our fans like to know who is in the team and who is not, I think it is more beneficial for us to keep these things quiet. I hope our supporters understand this view, as they want what is best for Liverpool. Barry Venison was also out of today's third-round FA Cup game at Second Division Stoke City; he is still

▼ John Barnes is tackled by Stoke's Brian Talbot during the FA Cup third-round goalless draw at the Victoria Ground.

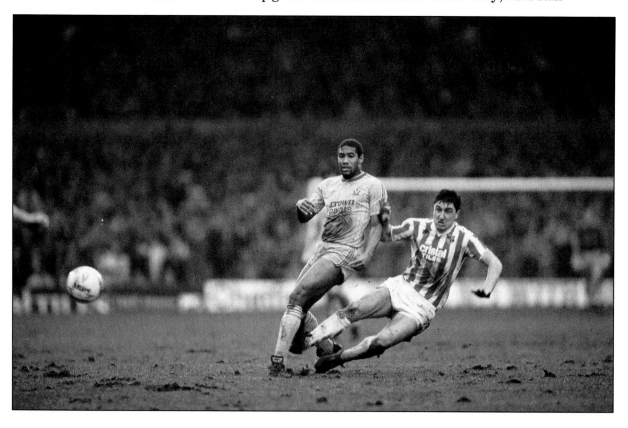

▲▶*John Barnes goes sprawling under challenge from Stoke City's George Berry.*

STOKE CITY	LIVERPOOL
FA Cup	**Victoria Ground**
9 January	**31,979**
STOKE 0	
LIVERPOOL 0	

STOKE	LIVERPOOL
Barrett	Hooper
Dixon	Gillespie
Carr	Lawrenson
Talbot	Nicol
Bould	Whelan
Berry	Hansen
Ford	Beardsley
Henry	Aldridge
Morgan	Houghton
Stainrod	Barnes
Parkin	McMahon

SUBSTITUTES:	
Shaw	Johnston
Daly	Spackman

▼ *Goalkeeper Mike Hooper, who crowned an impressive performance at Stoke with this late save from Graham Shaw.*

suffering from the calf injury he sustained against Coventry on New Year's Day.

Mike Hooper replaced Bruce and Mark Lawrenson came into the defence at left-back with Steve Nicol switching to the right in a mud-bath contest. Mike did tremendously well as our last line of defence, handling the ball with confidence, taking crosses cleanly and producing a superb save four minutes from the end when he raced out to prevent Stoke substitute Graham Shaw from scoring. That ensured the game finished goalless, setting up an Anfield replay next Tuesday. The fact that the underdogs had a late chance should not be exaggerated. Games should be judged on 90 minutes and overriding all other considerations is that Mike was equal to the task of making the save.

Ronnie Whelan's booking today for a foul on Simon Stainrod was only our fourth first-team caution of the season.

Tuesday, 12 January: Yesterday's fourth-round FA Cup draw gave us or Stoke a trip to Second Division leaders Aston Villa. But we still had a job to do in tonight's replay. With Bruce and Barry still unfit our only changes against Stoke were positional, with John Barnes switching to attack down the right flank and Ray Houghton moving to the left. It would be something different for Stoke to contend with and I thought it was worth a try.

It was another hard game, just like Saturday's, but we created a host of chances. I counted fifteen reasonable opportunities we made for ourselves, yet the match was won and lost by a single goal from Peter Beardsley in the ninth

minute. A cross from John Barnes was headed by Berry into Peter's path and although he appeared to mishit his shot the ball bounced and looped over Stoke goalkeeper Scott Barrett and into the Kop net. It does not matter how they go in – they all count. Peter deserves credit for being there to take the opportunity. As his opponent Berry said after the match: 'You only see him in fleeting glances . . . you've got him and then he goes in places you don't want him to be.'

Our progress to round four means that the game at Aston Villa will be switched to Sunday, 31 January, and screened live by ITV.

LIVERPOOL	STOKE CITY

FA Cup	Anfield
12 January	**39,147**

LIVERPOOL 1 (Beardsley)

STOKE 0

LIVERPOOL	STOKE
Hooper	Barrett
Gillespie	Dixon
Lawrenson	Carr
Nicol	Talbot
Whelan	Bould
Hansen	Berry
Beardsley	Ford
Aldridge	Henry
Houghton	Morgan
Barnes	Stainrod
McMahon	Parkin
SUBSTITUTES:	
Johnston	Shaw
Spackman	Daly

◀▼Ronnie Whelan is tackled by Stoke's Tony Ford during the FA Cup replay at Anfield which was settled by an early strike from Peter Beardsley – the only goal of the match and of the tie.

97

Thursday, 14 January: The club today unveiled a sponsorship deal that was the best of all worlds for Liverpool and our fans. It was announced by our chairman John Smith at an Anfield Press conference that the Italian-owned domestic appliance company Candy had agreed a £1 million three-year sponsorship starting from next season. They will succeed Crown Paints, who have backed us for six years, and I am delighted that Candy are to continue the sponsorship process which Liverpool introduced to the Football League by linking up with Hitachi in 1979.

Candy is a major European company with a strong local, Merseyside identity – their United Kingdom headquarters are at Bromborough. Many of their employees are among our supporters, so it is very satisfying that their company is supporting us in this way as we try to do our best for Merseyside. The fact that Candy is an Italian firm cannot be overlooked either. It shows that despite the horrific events of Heysel the bridge-building process between our countries is moving powerfully forward. And whisper it . . . the company that sponsors Juventus and whose name Ian Rush now wears on his shirt is Ariston, Candy's business rivals!

▼ *A new name for next season: our captain Alan Hansen, John Aldridge, John Barnes, Ronnie Whelan, Ray Houghton and Peter Beardsley model our strip bearing the name of our new sponsors Candy.*

Saturday, 16 January: It was estimated that 250 million TV viewers worldwide saw – or will see on recordings – our 2-0 win over Arsenal today. If they react in a similar fashion to most of the 44,000-plus spectators at Anfield they will be standing to applaud two superb goals which were masterpieces for different reasons. We were into the last half-minute of the first half and the ball was seemingly running into touch in the Arsenal half. But Steve McMahon not only showed marvellous determination to keep it in play but fed Peter Beardsley whose pass gave John Aldridge the chance to put us in front with his twentieth goal of the season. Then after 61 minutes Peter Beardsley showed dazzling skills when he nutmegged Arsenal substitute Michael Thomas and, as goalkeeper John Lukic came out and committed himself by going down for the shot, Peter just 'chipped' him for a magnificent goal.

It had all of us in the dug-out punching the air in delight and appreciation. What a way for Peter to start the celebrations for his twenty-seventh birthday on Monday! It was his fourth goal in as many matches but, in addition to his ability to score goals as stunning as that, he contributes so much to the team effort, which is exactly why we made such a big investment in him.

The goals crowned an entertaining afternoon and the

LIVERPOOL	ARSENAL

First Division	Anfield
16 January	**44,294**

LIVERPOOL 2 (Aldridge, Beardsley)

ARSENAL 0

LIVERPOOL	ARSENAL
Hooper	Lukic
Gillespie	Winterburn
Lawrenson	Sansom
Nicol	Williams
Whelan	Caesar
Hansen	Adams
Beardsley	Rocastle
Aldridge	Hayes
Houghton	Smith
Barnes	Quinn
McMahon	Richardson

SUBSTITUTES:	
Johnston	Groves
Spackman	Thomas

◀ *Ronnie Whelan stretches for the ball as Arsenal goalkeeper John Lukic races out to save.*

▲ *A well-known face in his new role of match commentator. French superstar Michel Platini donned the headphones at Anfield for our League game against Arsenal.*

▼ ▶ *Arsenal defender Tony Adams tussles with his England colleague Peter Beardsley during the First Division duel at Anfield which will be remembered for two marvellous goals, both for us. Peter 'nutmegs' Arsenal's Michael Thomas before scoring the second one in our 2-0 win.*

impeccable behaviour of the supporters, witnessed by such huge numbers around the world, was another positive advertisement for English football. Among the television contingent present was French superstar Michel Platini, who is now an analyst for a cable TV company in France. At the after-match Press conference I was asked about Platini fitting into this Liverpool team. I replied: 'If I can't get a game, he can't!' Certainly the lads are bombing along. This was our twenty-third League game unbeaten and Nottingham Forest's home draw with Charlton means that we are fifteen points clear at the top.

The only disappointment of the afternoon was another injury to Mark Lawrenson, who had reverted to right-back today with Steve Nicol returning to the left. Mark had to go off six minutes after the interval following a kick above his Achilles, which meant another stint of first-team action for versatile Nigel Spackman as a straight replacement.

Tuesday, 19 January: Our reserve match against Hull at Anfield tonight gave Bruce Grobbelaar the opportunity of playing through 90 minutes after missing the last three games because of a gashed leg. It was also a chance for me to have a taste of action again at Anfield, my first appearance on our pitch since I played in Ian Rush's farewell game against Watford last May.

A crowd of 1200 turned out to see us win 4-1 and Bruce came through unscathed. I also finished the match, which was my first full 90 minutes since that Watford game last season, and I enjoyed it. But how often I play will depend on circumstances. I felt I needed a game and this was the right opportunity. I will have other games if it is beneficial for me to play, but I am not going to stand in the way of a youngster or somebody who needs a run-out after injury.

Saturday, 23 January: Mark Lawrenson's absence with the Achilles injury he received against Arsenal coincided today with Barry Venison's return to fitness after a three-match absence with calf trouble; he came back into the side at right-back against Charlton at Selhurst Park.

However, I had a straight choice to make between goalkeepers Bruce Grobbelaar and Mike Hooper, who had played so capably in the three previous matches when Bruce had been ruled out with an infected leg gash. Today Bruce was fit enough to play if he had to. But I felt it was not necessary to take the risk and at the same time I had every faith in Mike, so he stayed in as our last line of defence and again did well to keep a clean sheet in our 2-0 win. This result equalled the club record of eight consecutive clean sheets which had been set in 1920 and achieved again in 1974. Bruce and Mike have played four games each in the eight-game run matching that feat and it reflects great credit on them as well as underlining the quality of our defence, which has been largely unsung in a season when our forwards, quite understandably, have been constantly in the limelight.

Our defence had to be alert today because Charlton put us under heavy pressure early in the game. Our lads coped with it well, though, and we took the lead through Peter Beardsley on the half-hour with John Barnes adding a second after an hour. Our win put us seventeen points clear at the top and we have now gone twenty-four League games unbeaten. But it is sad to see Charlton at the bottom of the First Division. They contributed tremendously to a great game at Anfield in September which we won by the odd goal in five and they are a team that likes to try to play football. I have always found them a pleasant club and, personally, I hope they get out of

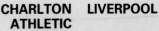

CHARLTON ATHLETIC	LIVERPOOL

First Division	Selhurst Park
23 January	28,095

CHARLTON 0

LIVERPOOL 2 (Beardsley, Barnes)

CHARLTON	LIVERPOOL
Bolder	Hooper
Humphrey	Gillespie
Reid	Venison
Mackenzie	Nicol
Shirtliff	Whelan
Thompson	Hansen
Bennett	Beardsley
Campbell	Aldridge
Jones	Houghton
Lee	Barnes
Mortimer	McMahon

SUBSTITUTES:

Gritt	Johnston
Crooks	Spackman

▶ *Steve McMahon tussles with Charlton's David Campbell during our 2-0 win at Selhurst Park.*

relegation trouble and stay up. We did not give them any help towards that aim today and their manager Lennie Lawrence lost his bet that Charlton would beat us. At least his club's bank balance is healthier thanks to the bumper crowd of 28,095 which was the biggest attendance at Selhurst Park – the ground Charlton share with Crystal Palace – since 1980. It broke the ground receipts record of more than £100,000 and was Charlton's largest crowd since their days at The Valley in 1977. While our lads are winning it is nice to know that they are also entertaining people and attracting the public.

Tuesday, 26 January: Our reserve team had a very satisfying 3-0 win over Derby County in tonight's Central League fixture at Anfield, satisfying because it was virtually Derby's first team! Nine of their players figured in the First Division game at Anfield in September when we won 4-0. Derby contacted us to ask if we had any objections to their parading a stronger than usual line-up tonight and we said we had none. The team they chose was: Wallington, Sage,

Forsyth, Williams, Wright, Blades, Lewis, Garner, Gee, Gregory, Callaghan. Substitutes: McClaren, Penney.

In the event, it was a very useful outing for our team, which itself included some fair players! Paul Walsh scored two of our goals and hit the bar, and John Durnin also got on the scoresheet on a satisfying night that saw Bruce Grobbelaar come through his second reserve outing since his last senior game, against Coventry on New Year's Day. Jan Molby continued his comeback after being out first with a broken foot and, latterly, through ankle damage, and Kevin MacDonald played for us after returning from his loan spell at Leicester.

Saturday, 30 January: Our youth team did well today – they progressed into the quarter-finals of the FA Youth Cup with a 1-0 Anfield win over a highly-rated Derby County side. This competition is as big and important to youth coach John Bennison, youth development officer Malcolm Cook and the youngsters as the FA Cup is to the first-team squad and staff.

The main aim of having junior teams is to develop young talent, but if you enter any competition it is better to do well in it than not to. It is good, therefore, to see the youth team reach the last eight of their national competition following their impressive defeat of holders Coventry in the previous round. A John Fagan goal two minutes from the end saw the lads through. The other important factor from their point of view is that playing in the Youth Cup gives them rare opportunities of appearing at Anfield, because their A and B matches are staged at the training ground.

Sunday, 31 January: Part of the manager's job is making decisions and you try to make the best you can for purely professional reasons. Today I decided to recall Bruce Grobbelaar in goal for our live televised fourth-round FA Cup tie at Aston Villa. That meant deep disappointment for Mike Hooper, which is totally understandable. The first to know my decision were the two people involved, Bruce and Mike. And in telling them I could sympathize with Mike's feelings; he had played so well in his four-match stint during which nothing had got past him. But he is not twenty-four until next month – still relatively young for a goalkeeper – and the way he has performed has certainly been of benefit to his career, has helped Liverpool and, in a way, Bruce as well.

During my years at Liverpool reserve goalkeepers have had little opportunity to display their talents at first-team level because of the form, consistency and freedom from injury of the man in possession. Peter McDonnell left the club in 1978

ASTON VILLA	LIVERPOOL

FA Cup	Villa Park
31 January	46,324

ASTON VILLA 0

LIVERPOOL 2 (Barnes, Beardsley)

ASTON VILLA	LIVERPOOL
Spink	Grobbelaar
Gage	Ablett
Gallacher	Venison
Gray	Nicol
Evans	Spackman
Keown	Hansen
Birch	Beardsley
Lillis	Aldridge
Thompson	Houghton
Daley	Barnes
McInally	McMahon

SUBSTITUTES:
Aspinall	Johnston
Norton	Molby

▶ *Peter Beardsley's trickery gave Aston Villa's defence plenty to think about in the FA Cup tie at Villa Park.*

without making a single senior appearance in his four years as deputy to Ray Clemence. Steve Ogrizovic had only slightly more opportunities, and played five times in the first team when Ray was injured. But since moving on to Coventry, via Shrewsbury, Steve has distinguished himself, forced his way into the England reckoning and earned a place in Bobby Robson's Football League squad for the centenary game against the Rest of the World at the start of this season.

Another of our reserve keepers, Bob Wardle, sadly had to quit the game through injury but yet another, Bob Bolder, who never made a first-team appearance for us, has been playing brilliantly for Charlton and winning tremendous praise. In his case – and Steve's – being at Liverpool does not seem to have done them any harm and might have helped their careers elsewhere. It is all about opportunity and how people respond to it if and when it comes. Mike Hooper has taken his with both hands – literally – and has now had seventeen first-team outings for us. We now know that the strength of our squad extends to having two first-class goalkeepers and Bruce Grobbelaar is well aware that he faces a stern challenge for his position.

Today, however, Bruce was back and played his part in another impressive team performance that brought us a 2-0 win in front of a 46,000-plus Villa Park crowd, a place in the fifth round and a club record ninth consecutive clean sheet. Recalling Bruce was my decision; but we were forced to make two other team changes because Gary Gillespie was unfit after tearing a thigh muscle in training last Friday and Ronnie Whelan was ruled out with a knee injury. We did not publicize these injuries because we felt that would not be right for Liverpool. There was a chance that if Villa had advance knowledge that we would be without these two players it could have been to their advantage; so we did not disclose it. The media might not like it but my first responsibility is to Liverpool Football Club and, as I have said, I hope our supporters will fully understand and back my policy in these matters.

Having lost Gary and Ronnie, I decided to pair Steve Nicol with Alan Hansen at the centre of defence – a partnership that had looked impressive when they played together for the Anglo-Scots against home-based Scots in my testimonial match at Hampden Park in May 1986 – bring in Gary Ablett to start his first match of the season at left-back and draft Nigel Spackman into midfield. The value of players like Steve Nicol and Nigel Spackman is beyond assessment. They are the sort who will not only do a job for you virtually anywhere, but do a very good job. Versatility is a talent in itself and Steve has played in every position for us except goalkeeper and up front; and I am sure he would acquit himself well in attack if we asked him to. Nigel is also proving a great utility player since his signing from Chelsea last February. That was £400,000 well spent.

Both Steve and Nigel did well for us today. A rare header from John Barnes – just to remind his former Watford boss Graham Taylor that his head is part of his armoury – put us in front after 53 minutes. Our win was clinched by Peter Beardsley's 100th senior club goal, his tenth of the season for us, and his sixth in as many matches. It was our thirtieth game of the season in all competitions and we have lost only one. So we are well pleased at the way things are going.

DIVISION ONE

		Home					Away					
	P	W	D	L	F	A	W	D	L	F	A	Pts
Liverpool	24	12	1	0	36	3	7	4	0	23	8	62
Nottm For	24	6	3	2	25	9	7	3	3	21	12	45
Man Utd	25	6	5	1	18	11	6	4	3	20	14	45
Everton	25	9	2	1	23	5	3	5	5	13	11	43
Arsenal	26	7	2	4	23	11	5	4	4	14	14	42
Wimbledon	25	6	5	2	21	13	5	2	5	18	17	40
QPR	25	7	3	3	19	11	4	4	4	11	17	40
Luton	24	7	4	3	22	11	3	1	6	10	15	35
Sheff Wed	25	7	1	5	18	16	3	3	6	13	22	34
Tottenham	26	7	2	4	19	15	2	4	7	7	16	33
Southmptn	25	4	4	4	15	15	4	4	5	18	21	32
Newcastle	24	4	4	4	13	14	4	4	4	17	21	32
Chelsea	26	6	6	0	18	10	2	1	11	13	32	31
West Ham	25	4	5	4	15	16	3	4	5	13	18	30
Portsmth	26	3	7	4	16	18	2	4	6	8	24	26
Norwich	25	4	2	6	17	18	3	2	8	6	15	25
Coventry	23	2	4	4	10	17	4	3	6	14	21	25
Derby	23	3	3	5	10	10	3	3	6	10	18	24
Oxford	24	5	1	6	19	24	1	4	7	10	22	23
Watford	25	3	3	6	8	13	2	4	7	9	19	22
Charlton	25	3	4	6	12	18	1	4	7	11	20	20

FEBRUARY

Monday, 1 February, 1988: The FA Cup fifth-round draw gave us an away game at either Everton or Middlesbrough, who face a replay after drawing 1-1 at Goodison. Inevitably, Merseyside is already talking of another derby game but all we can do is await the outcome of the replay. Anyway, the FA Cup has to be put on ice for a few weeks because we have important League games coming up first.

Tuesday, 2 February: It was revealed in the Press today that the Scottish FA are to create a special Soccer Hall of Fame to honour all Scotland's international players who have collected fifty or more caps. I was privileged to wear a Scotland jersey on 102 occasions, yet the pride I felt is no lesser or greater than that of a player who has won just one cap. It is nice to see the SFA recognizing players who have served their country and, although it will be disappointing to those who have fallen short of fifty caps, a line had to be drawn somewhere.

The idea, I understand, is for every player with a half-century of caps or more to be known as a 'Scottish Honour Player' and they are to be presented with a commemorative gold medal before this season's Scottish Cup Final. We will also be guests of the SFA for Scotland's home games at Hampden Park for the rest of our lives and there is to be a 'Scottish Honour Players' Room' at SFA headquarters in Glasgow.

The SFA deserve to be congratulated for this practical recognition and I look forward to meeting the other players, past and present, whose contributions are being saluted. They are: Danny McGrain (62 caps), Denis Law (55), Willie Miller (55), Billy Bremner (54), Graeme Souness (54), George Young (53), Alan Rough (53), Joe Jordan (52), Asa Hartford (50), Alex McLeish (50).

Saturday, 6 February: We still do not know who we are to play in the FA Cup fifth round because Middlesbrough and Everton drew 2-2 at Ayresome Park on Wednesday night and will return to Goodison Park on Tuesday for a third meeting.

For only the second time this season we failed to score in a League game – today's home match with West Ham finished goalless. The only other First Division match in which we failed to score was also at Anfield, against Norwich in

LIVERPOOL	WEST HAM UNITED

First Division	Anfield
6 February	42,049

LIVERPOOL 0

WEST HAM 0

LIVERPOOL	WEST HAM
Grobbelaar	McAlister
Ablett	Stewart
Venison	Ince
Nicol	Bonds
Spackman	Strodder
Hansen	Gale
Beardsley	Ward
Aldridge	Brady
Houghton	Dickens
Barnes	Cottee
McMahon	Robson

SUBSTITUTES:

Johnston	McQueen
Molby	Keen

▶ *Nigel Spackman and West Ham's Billy Bonds tussling for possession.*

▲▶ *John Aldridge challenges Gary Strodder and, then, heads past the West Ham defender. But the London club kept us goalless at Anfield.*

November. Our 'blank' today was down to a mixture of Tom McAlister's fine goalkeeping and our own failure to put away the chances we had.

McAlister made a string of impressive saves against attempts by Ray Houghton, John Barnes, John Aldridge and Peter Beardsley and, try as we did, we just could not break through. We tried a late reshuffle by bringing on Craig Johnston for John Aldridge and pushed John Barnes down the middle. But West Ham, who again deployed midfielder Stewart Robson at right-back against Barnesie, held out for a point – the second they have taken against us this season.

Sometimes on days like these you get the benefit of a mis-kick in front of goal or a lucky bounce. It clearly was not our day and Steve McMahon was unfortunate to be booked by referee Jim McAulay for dissent, the result of a misunderstanding about where we should take a free kick. Steve Nicol was also booked – for a foul on Tony Cottee – bringing our total of cautions so far to six.

▼ *John Barnes shields the ball from Stewart Robson.*

While our attack had an unusually barren afternoon our defence extended the club record number of consecutive clean sheets to ten as we registered our twenty-fifth League game of the season unbeaten. The team was unchanged from the Cup win at Villa, with Steve Nicol again partnering Alan Hansen at the centre of defence in the absence of Gary Gillespie, and Gary Ablett at left-back; and once again it looked an efficient unit. This was our last home game until 12 March when we are scheduled to play Wimbledon. But that is also FA Cup sixth-round day so the fixture could change and prolong our absence from Anfield. We still have twenty home games and twenty away in the League and you have to take what comes in cup competitions.

Before today's kickoff I was presented, on the pitch, with my third Bells Manager of the Month Award this season – a gallon of Bells whisky and a cheque for £250. Although I was the one to receive these awards the whole of the squad and the backroom staff have, by their contributions, earned them too. I see my role as supplying the lads with a bit of guidance now and again.

▼ *Receiving the Bells Manager of the Month Award before our home game with West Ham.*

▼ *A duel between Steve McMahon and Paul Ince.*

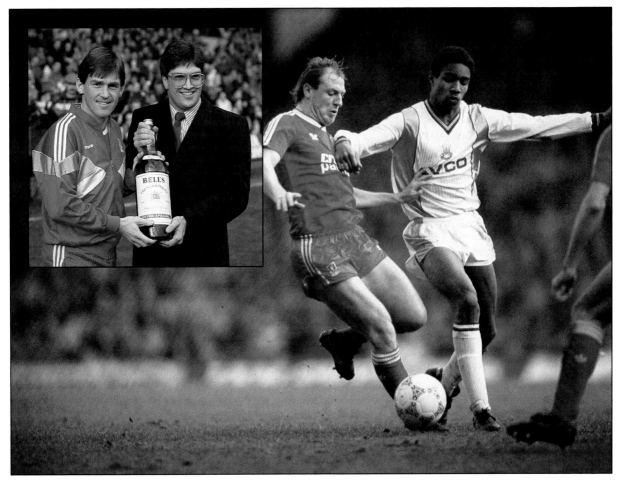

Monday, 8 February: Everyone at the club was delighted today for Steve McMahon who won his first call-up to the England squad, for next week's friendly in Israel. And he has achieved international recognition the only way a player can – by playing well for his club. Steve's reaction underlines what a family Anfield is. 'I've got to thank everyone at the club including the three tea ladies who make me tea and toast every morning,' he said. 'They kept encouraging me and told me I'd play for England.'

Tuesday, 9 February: At last we know who our fifth-round FA Cup opponents will be. Everton beat Middlesbrough 2-1 in tonight's second replay at Goodison to set up another Mersey derby engagement which, almost inevitably, will be screened live on television a week on Sunday. Just like the Littlewoods Cup, in which we also met Everton back in October, it means that one of the FA Cup favourites has to go out. Merseyside would rather see this tie take place at Wembley, but the rest of the country will not be unhappy at the fact that either us or Everton has to go out.

Wednesday, 10 February: A newspaper story has reported that I am in line to be the new manager of Barcelona, saying that 'allegedly' I have already been approached by somebody acting for the Barcelona president. It is absolute nonsense and does not contain a shred of truth. The word 'allegedly' kills the story stone dead. I also took exception to the assertion that I would have language problems in Spain. I think I've done all right coping with English since I moved here from Celtic in 1977!

Saturday, 13 February: With our injury situation unchanged, the team that was held to a goalless draw by West Ham a week ago today thrashed Watford 4-1 on a Vicarage Road quagmire illustrating, perhaps, that the difference between scoring and not scoring can be wafer-thin.

Watford tested Bruce Grobbelaar early in the game and he responded with a brilliant save from Trevor Senior's powerful shot to prevent us falling behind. Two goals from Peter Beardsley – bringing his total to eight in as many matches since New Year's Day – a side-foot from John Aldridge to take his total to twenty-one this season and another from John Barnes ensured our ninth four-goal tally in the League, which indicates how well the boys have been playing. Barnesie celebrated his return to Watford with a goal scored on the hour which put us 4-0 ahead, and it is nice to observe that his transfer to us has left no hint of animosity between John and

WATFORD	LIVERPOOL

First Division	**Vicarage Road**
13 February	**23,838**

WATFORD 1 (Blissett)

LIVERPOOL 4 (Beardsley 2, Aldridge, Barnes)

WATFORD	LIVERPOOL
Coton	Grobbelaar
Gibbs	Ablett
Rostron	Venison
Jackett	Nicol
Morris	Spackman
McClelland	Hansen
Sterling	Beardsley
Allen	Aldridge
Senior	Houghton
Porter	Barnes
Sherwood	McMahon

SUBSTITUTES:	
Blissett	Johnston
Pullan	Molby

▲ *Our goalkeeper Bruce Grobbelaar spots foreign spies in the shape of the Monaco team who have a front-row view of our 4-1 win at Watford. Glenn Hoddle and Mark Hateley, who have teamed up with the French League club, are in the centre of the row.*

▶ *Peter Beardsley scores his second goal at Vicarage Road.*

his former club or their supporters. I said publicly yesterday that the Vicarage Road fans would give him a nice reception and I was proved correct.

Our win was Watford's first defeat in six League and Cup games under their new manager Steve Harrison, the man who succeeded Dave Bassett, but not before an unusual thing happened – we conceded our first goal of 1988, in fact our first since the 2-2 draw at Southampton on 12 December. Luther Blissett scored it 15 minutes from the end and our lads, who have done so tremendously well in setting a new club record of ten consecutive clean sheets, were annoyed with themselves for conceding it. Their attitude says a great deal about their standards.

Our decision to give John Barnes and Steve McMahon a breather for the last 11 minutes because of their involvement in next week's England match in Israel meant a significant first senior appearance of the season for Jan Molby, who went on as substitute with Craig Johnston. Jan has had a deeply frustrating seven months, first with a broken bone in his foot and then ankle damage. The game was significant for our reserve centre-back Alex Watson, who was included in the squad, although not in the final thirteen, for the first time since he was an unused substitute in the Littlewoods Cup game at Fulham in October 1986. Alex, brother of Everton and England centre-half Dave, is still only nineteen and his inclusion in the party is a reflection of the impressive progress he is making in our Central League team. Paul Walsh also travelled south with us for weekend transfer talks with Tottenham, after the clubs had agreed a fee of £500,000.

Monday, 15 February: Paul had more talks with Tottenham manager Terry Venables and telephoned me, as promised, to inform me that he had decided to sign for them. I told him we were sorry to lose him but wished him all the best and he made his debut in tonight's friendly against Monaco at White Hart Lane. I believe Tottenham have got a very good player at a very fair price and it could well turn out that they have got the better of the deal. We took a bit of a chance in allowing Paul to go because it has depleted the attacking strength of our squad. At the same time, however, we felt we could not stand in his way because we appreciate that a player of his talents should be playing at a higher level than that afforded here, where he has been kept out of the team this season by Peter Beardsley, an England regular, and the First Division's top scorer John Aldridge.

At twenty-five, though, Paul has the time and the talent to reclaim the place he won in the England team before he joined us from Luton in 1984 and I feel certain he will do a good job for Tottenham. During his period at Liverpool he made a substantial contribution to our historic League and FA Cup double success of 1986, scoring twelve goals in his twenty-two appearances, a record he can be proud of. Paul was injured against Manchester United in February of that year and, subsequently, made just one League appearance and one in the Screen Sport Super Cup before the end of that season. But nobody at this club will forget the part he played in our Double win.

Tuesday, 16 February: I was there to welcome another addition to the Dalglish team at around 2.30 this morning when my wife Marina gave birth to a beautiful 7lb 11oz daughter called Lauren. I am now well and truly outnumbered by females, because we also have two other daughters – twelve-year-old Kelly and six-year-old Lynsey. That leaves Paul, our eleven-year-old son, and me facing impossible odds!

Seriously, though, we are all delighted at our new arrival, and mother and daughter are doing splendidly. Babies are a way of life at Anfield right now with about eight of them expected during the next few months. One of our players, Gary Gillespie, and his wife Susan are expecting twins in May, and the wife of our physiotherapist Paul Chadwick is also pregnant.

Sunday, 21 February: Congratulations to Steve McMahon. On Wednesday he won his first England cap in their rain-lashed 1-1 draw with Israel at Tel Aviv's Ramat Gan Stadium, a venue we have played at several times in friendly matches.

We came out on top in today's live televised FA Cup tussle with Everton at Goodison Park by the only goal of the game – a rare and ironic one from Ray Houghton. Rare because Ray disclosed that it was his first headed goal in senior football and ironic because he was the match winner in the number nine jersey made so famous by Ian Rush, the all-time record derby-match scorer with nineteen goals during his Liverpool

▼ *Barry Venison outjumps Everton's Neil Pointon and Paul Power.*

EVERTON	LIVERPOOL
FA Cup	Goodison Park
21 February	48,270

EVERTON 0

LIVERPOOL 1 (Houghton)

EVERTON	LIVERPOOL
Southall	Grobbelaar
Stevens	Ablett
Pointon	Venison
Van Den Hauwe	Nicol
Watson	Spackman
Reid	Hansen
Steven	Beardsley
Heath	Aldridge
Sharp	Houghton
Snodin	Barnes
Power	McMahon

SUBSTITUTES:

Bracewell	Johnston
Harper	Molby

▼ *Ray Houghton beats Everton's Paul Power to head the only goal of the FA Cup fifth-round tie.*

career. And Ian, having a weekend off from Juventus duties, happened to be watching from the Press Box.

It was a typical derby of few chances with an extra edge of tension because it was a cup tie. Remarkably, it was the tenth meeting of the two clubs in cup competitions in less than four years, including five encounters in the finals of the FA Cup, Milk Cup and Screen Sport Super Cup and two Charity Shield matches as well as our Littlewoods Cup ties.

The goal that took us into the quarter-finals came 15 minutes from the end after great determination by Peter Beardsley forced Everton to concede a throw-in on their right. Gary Ablett threw to John Barnes, who played a one-two with Peter before delivering the cross for Ray Houghton to beat the Everton defence and head past Neville Southall. Our last three signings – Ray, Peter and John – created and executed the move and it was pleasing to see them involved in this way. We were short on players last summer and my view was that we might as well buy good ones. That is what we got in this trio, who also happen to be positive people in their attitude and outlook. So we have been doubly fortunate.

John Barnes gave his room-mate Peter Beardsley an almighty shock in the hotel before the match. He told him he was going for a shave and came back looking like Marvin Hagler after shaving his head! The first I knew about it was when I saw the 'new look' Barnesie as he got on the team bus to leave for Goodison. I didn't pass any comment. I couldn't think of anything to say!

◀ *A 'good-luck' handshake between me and Everton assistant manager Terry Darracott – watched by Colin Harvey – before the FA Cup derby at Goodison.*

Monday, 22 February: The FA Cup quarter-final draw pitched us into a Maine Road visit to Manchester City, the fifth time in succession our number has come out of the bag as the away team since we had to go to Luton in last season's third round. But you have to accept what you are given and our reward for defeating Everton was just to be in the draw. The game at City is – and this is no surprise – to be televised live. I think we are on TV more than *EastEnders*! It doesn't worry me. Some people have asked whether our television exposure gives other managers and teams an advantage because they have seen what we can do. The tense is important here. They might have seen what we *have* done but they have no idea what we are *going* to do.

Saturday, 27 February: We extended our unbeaten First Division sequence to twenty-seven games at Portsmouth today without producing anything like our best football. We were fortunate that Mick Quinn missed a couple of good early chances for Portsmouth and luck was with us again four minutes after the interval to help us take the lead. John Barnes put in a cross that deflected off Portsmouth defender Billy Gilbert and looped over goalkeeper Alan Knight into the net. However, there was no fortune about our second goal, also scored by Barnesie, five minutes from the end. It was well worked. Peter Beardsley beat Kevin Ball and Paul Handyman on the right before crossing for Ray Houghton to lay the ball into John's path for his twelfth goal of the season.

PORTSMTH	LIVERPOOL

First Division	**Fratton Park**
27 February	**28,117**

PORTSMOUTH 0
LIVERPOOL 2 (Barnes 2)

PORTSMTH	LIVERPOOL
Knight	Grobbelaar
Gilbert	Ablett
Sandford	Venison
Dillon	Nicol
Blake	Spackman
Ball	Hansen
Horne	Beardsley
Fillery	Aldridge
Quinn	Houghton
Connor	Barnes
Hilaire	McMahon

SUBSTITUTES:	
Hardyman	Whelan
Baird	Molby

We are grateful that we have gained another three points, extended our unbeaten run and kept another clean sheet without having given one of our better displays. Right-back Barry Venison, who played in an unchanged team, complained of calf trouble after the match, so instead of travelling to Spain for next Tuesday's testimonial match against Osasuna, for our former midfielder Sammy Lee, he will go back home for treatment.

The only change in our line-up today was at substitute level, where Ronnie Whelan, out of the side for the previous four games with knee damage, took over from Craig Johnston on the bench alongside Jan Molby. Craig hurt his knee in training during the week so we left him behind. I again included Alex Watson in the party to travel to Portsmouth and on to Spain on Monday morning. I also called up our eighteen-year-old youth team captain Charlie Boyd, a midfielder or full-back who has been impressive both at youth and reserve team level. And Kevin MacDonald was named in the squad for the first time since he broke his left leg at Southampton back in September 1986 and it is terrific to have him available again.

▼ *John Barnes leaps over grounded Portsmouth goalkeeper Alan Knight during our 2-0 win at Fratton Park.*

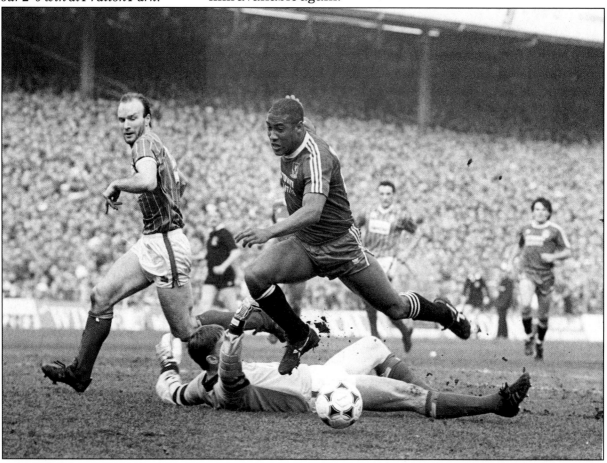

▲ *In full voice – that's me trying to encourage the lads at Portsmouth.*

Sunday, 28 February: A Sunday newspaper has reported that I refused permission for Craig Johnston to join the England squad for the game in Israel the week before last so that he could play in our reserves. This is totally untrue. Bobby Robson never even asked me if Craig could join his England party. If he had, there would have been no problem.

On the weekend before the Israel match I spoke to England coach Don Howe on the telephone. He said their squad had been hit by injuries and that Bobby would be getting in touch with me to ask for Craig. I gave Don my home phone number and waited for a call from the England manager. It never came. I would like to know who provided such erroneous information for the newspaper story.

Monday, 29 February: After staying over the weekend in a Surrey hotel we flew to Spain today for tomorrow's game against Osasuna in the northern Basque city of Pamplona, famous for its running of the bulls. I hope our red jerseys also attract as many people as possible to make it a rewarding testimonial match for Sammy Lee.

		Home					Away					
DIVISION ONE												
	P	W	D	L	F	A	W	D	L	F	A	Pts
Liverpool	**27**	**12**	**2**	**0**	**36**	**3**	**9**	**4**	**0**	**29**	**9**	**69**
Man Utd	29	7	5	1	19	11	8	5	3	25	17	55
Nottm For	26	7	3	2	28	11	7	4	3	22	13	49
Everton	27	11	2	1	26	5	3	5	5	13	11	49
Arsenal	28	9	2	4	29	12	5	4	4	14	14	48
QPR	28	9	3	3	22	11	4	4	5	11	19	46
Wimbledon	28	6	6	2	21	13	5	3	6	19	19	42
Luton	26	8	4	3	29	15	3	1	7	11	17	38
Tottenham	29	7	3	4	20	16	3	5	7	10	16	38
Sheff Wed	29	8	1	6	20	20	3	3	8	14	28	37
Newcastle	27	5	4	5	17	18	4	5	4	17	21	36
Southmptn	28	4	5	4	16	16	4	4	7	19	24	33
West Ham	28	4	6	4	16	17	3	5	6	13	19	32
Coventry	27	3	5	4	13	17	5	3	7	15	22	32
Chelsea	29	6	6	1	19	12	2	1	13	16	38	31
Norwich	28	4	3	6	17	18	4	3	8	9	16	30
Portsmth	29	4	7	5	18	21	2	5	6	9	25	30
Derby	27	4	3	6	12	12	3	4	7	11	20	28
Oxford	27	5	3	6	19	24	1	4	8	13	29	25
Charlton	29	4	5	6	16	20	1	4	9	11	26	24
Watford	28	3	3	8	9	18	2	5	7	9	19	23

MARCH

Tuesday, 1 March, 1988: Snow on the mountains, a chilly wind and torrential rain were our weather experience in northern Spain. But it was heart-warming to see an attendance of 12,000 turn out for Sammy Lee's testimonial match between us and his club Osasuna tonight. What made that crowd figure even more laudable was the fact that the game was screened live on local Basque television and I am delighted for Sammy that the match did attract so many people.

He was a great little servant to Liverpool, a Merseyside-born lad who personified what every single person who stands on the Kop dreams of – pulling on a Liverpool jersey and playing for the club. It was just a pity that neither Sammy, nor another of our former players Michael Robinson, also now with Osasuna, could figure in tonight's match. They were both suffering from knee injuries and had to sit and watch when they must have been itching to get into the action.

We won 2-0, with a first-half goal from Ray Houghton and one in the second half from yours truly. I had come on just after Ray's goal in place of John Aldridge, who had taken a kick on his thigh. We also had to withdraw Ronnie Whelan during the second half of his first game back following knee trouble. After being ruled out for four games we named him as a substitute at Portsmouth last Saturday but he did not go on, although we thought he had recovered from the injury. Now he is complaining of more pain in his knee so I hope it is nothing too serious. Ronnie's withdrawal gave nineteen-year-old centre-back Alex Watson a run-out in the second half, at the start of which we sent on Kevin MacDonald for Jan Molby.

It was terrific to see Kevin ploughing through the mud because it was his first action with the first team – albeit a testimonial – since he suffered a double fracture of his left leg in the First Division game at Southampton back in September 1986. Kevin has shown exemplary patience and determination to get fit again, battling back after two operations, and his appearance tonight followed several in the reserves and a loan spell with Leicester.

The man with the best idea on this trip was undoubtedly my former boss Bob Paisley, who came with us as one of our travelling directors complete with heavy overcoat. I think some other members of our party were willing to buy it off him when they realized that the city of Pamplona in March is hardly the Costa del Sol!

OSASUNA 0

LIVERPOOL 2 (Houghton, Dalglish)

Sammy Lee   **1 March**
Testimonial

LIVERPOOL

Grobbelaar	SUBSTITUTES:
Ablett	Boyd
Spackman	Beardsley
Nicol	Watson
Whelan	MacDonald
Hansen	Dalglish
Molby	
Aldridge	
Houghton	
Barnes	
McMahon	

Saturday, 5 March: It was my thirty-seventh birthday yesterday and I could have thought of better ways to celebrate than finding a batch of enforced absentees for a game at QPR. Thankfully, it was our last outing on the London club's plastic pitch before they rip it up and revert to grass at the end of the season. Despite the surface, and our injuries, we won 1-0 – our twenty-eighth consecutive First Division game unbeaten since the start of the season and one short of the Leeds United record set in 1974.

John Aldridge's thigh knock sustained in Spain and Ronnie Whelan's recurrence of knee trouble ruled out both players, while Barry Venison, having recovered from a calf injury, felt unwell before the match and had to pull out. Their absence, in addition to that of Gary Gillespie with his continuing thigh injury, Mark Lawrenson, plagued by Achilles trouble, and Jim Beglin, who is still striving for fitness after a broken leg, made it a test for the depth and resources of our squad, a test passed with flying colours.

I decided to call in Alex Watson for his debut to play alongside Alan Hansen at centre-back, switch Steve Nicol to right-back, recall Craig Johnston to midfield and push John Barnes up alongside Peter Beardsley in attack where John Aldridge was missing for the first time this season. Jan Molby and I were the substitutes but neither of us went on. During the match we shuffled our pack a little, also using Ray Houghton up front alongside Peter, and the lads did a sound job to get a good result on a surface none of us likes. I have never met a professional who does. If you could name me a single player who likes any other kind of plastic except credit

▼*An acrobatic salute from Bruce Grobbelaar for the John Barnes goal that gave us victory at Queens Park Rangers.*

QUEENS PARK RANGERS	LIVERPOOL

First Division	Loftus Road
5 March	**23,171**

QPR 0

LIVERPOOL 1 (Barnes)

QPR	LIVERPOOL
Seaman	Grobbelaar
Dawes	Ablett
Neill	Watson
Parker	Nicol
McDonald	Spackman
Maguire	Hansen
Maddix	Beardsley
Falco	Johnston
Byrne	Houghton
Fereday	Barnes
Kerslake	McMahon

SUBSTITUTES:

Coney	Dalglish
Fleming	Molby

cards I would be astonished. I am not against artificial surfaces for community use. The more chance that youngsters and the general public have for sporting outlets the better. But I see no reason why these pitches cannot be laid at training grounds rather than main stadiums. It is an unfair anomaly to have them at League club grounds, especially in a First Division with aspirations of renewed entry into Europe, where plastic pitches are not allowed!

At this moment there is a possibility that UEFA will lift the general European ban on English clubs next season, and QPR are one of the clubs involved in the struggle for a First Division leading place. QPR, English pioneers of plastic, are playing their matches on it for the last season, but it is still unfair on clubs who have to visit Loftus Road, just as I have always considered it an injustice that the random chance of a cup draw can send a team to play on an artificial surface. That undoubtedly gives the home side an added advantage.

The greatest indictment of plastic pitches, however, is their outlawing by Europe's governing body UEFA, who refuse permission for any of their competitive matches to be played on artificial surfaces. QPR have already fallen foul of this rule – they had to play their home games in the 1984-85 UEFA Cup at Arsenal's Highbury stadium – and perhaps that is a factor in their decision to rip up their synthetic surface. I, for one, am not sorry about that even though I can say that Liverpool's record on artificial surfaces is quite impressive. Today's win was our sixth in eight League games on the plastic at QPR and Luton.

One member of our squad was just delighted to play in today's match. In fact, Alex Watson would have been happy to make his debut on plasterboard! He grasped his first-team opportunity in impressive style and nobody got past him at the back. Inevitably, comparisons will be made between Alex and his brother Dave, of Everton and England. But Alex is his own man with his own identity and today he has shown everybody what potential he has, which was a bonus to our win ensured by a 34th-minute goal from John Barnes after Craig Johnston's shot had come back off QPR goalkeeper David Seaman.

Monday, 7 March: A telephone call to my home ensured an unexpectedly dramatic end to the day. Barry Venison, who had been at Anfield this morning, doubled up in agony after reaching home in Southport and the doctor ordered him to hospital right away with suspected appendicitis. But Barry had an extra problem! Apparently he does not wear pyjamas and was desperate to get a pair to take to hospital with him.

After contacting Gary Gillespie, who could not provide him with a pair, he phoned me and fortunately I was able to oblige.

Barry's wife Julie drove him round to my house and, complete with two pairs of pyjamas, I drove him to the hospital where his appendix problem was confirmed and operated on within an hour and a half. Barry has already been troubled by Achilles and calf injuries this season and this is more bad luck for the lad. We wish him all the best for a speedy recovery.

Wednesday, 9 March: The official opening of Ellesmere Port FC's new floodlights at their Thornton Road stadium tonight gave us the chance to give Gary Gillespie a run-out following his six-match absence with thigh muscle damage. We were happy to accept an invitation to send a team to meet the North West Counties League club, for whom our reserve team coach Phil Thompson's brother Ian plays.

Phil led a strong side, mainly comprising lads from his Central League team, and Gary played for an hour of the match which we won 4-2. He reported no problems with his thigh so he is in contention for a place in our sixth-round FA Cup tie at Manchester City on Sunday.

Thursday, 10 March: We are going to be without Ronnie Whelan for a little while longer. Today he underwent micro-surgery to repair knee damage he originally sustained at Charlton in January. We thought he had recovered and had named him as one of the substitutes for the League game at Portsmouth last month when he sat out the match. However, when he played against Osasuna in Sammy Lee's testimonial three days later it was evident that he was still troubled by the problem and we had to send on Alex Watson to replace him during the second half.

Obviously, we hope this operation will cure the trouble and we look forward to having him back in contention for a place as soon as possible.

Sunday, 13 March: A tremendous team performance by our lads gave us a 4-0 win over Manchester City in front of the ITV cameras at Maine Road and took us into the FA Cup semi-final . . .the club's twentieth in major competitions since 1976.

Everybody played well in a side that had Gary Gillespie returning in central defence alongside Alan Hansen, with Alex Watson and Jan Molby on the substitutes' bench. As well as Barry Venison and Ronnie Whelan, we were still without

MANCHESTER CITY	LIVERPOOL

FA Cup   Maine Road

13 March   44,047

MAN CITY 0

LIVERPOOL 4 (Houghton, Beardsley pen, Johnston, Barnes)

MAN CITY	LIVERPOOL
Stowell	Grobbelaar
Gidman	Gillespie
Hinchcliffe	Ablett
Brightwell	Nicol
Lake	Spackman
Redmond	Hansen
White	Beardsley
Stewart	Johnston
Varadi	Houghton
McNab	Barnes
Simpson	McMahon

SUBSTITUTES:

Scott	Watson
Seagraves	Molby

▶ *Two meaningful moments for Craig Johnston during our 4-0 FA Cup win at Manchester City. First, he is fouled by Paul Lake to earn the penalty from which Peter Beardsley scored our second goal. Then Craig evades City goalkeeper Mike Stowell before scoring our third goal.*

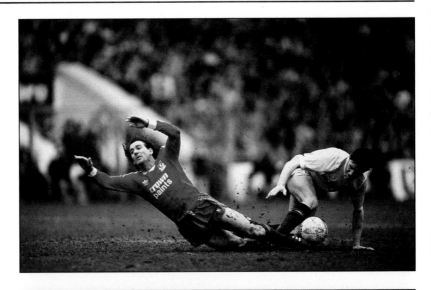

▼ *Braving a Manchester downpour: one of our Maine Road substitutes Alex Watson and reserve team coach Phil Thompson do their best to keep dry during our FA Cup sixth-round victory over Manchester City.*

John Aldridge. But Craig Johnston played up front with Peter Beardsley and did well, forcing Paul Lake to bundle him down for a penalty – from which Peter scored our second goal from the spot nine minutes into the second half – and scoring our third goal himself after 77 minutes.

We had gone into the lead in the 33rd minute with a goal very similar in creation to the one that took us through agairst Everton in the last round. Again, it was a combination of John Barnes and Peter Beardsley on the left, but this time Ray Houghton, who headed in Barnesie's cross at Everton, hooked the ball into the net at the near post. Gary Ablett, whose throw-in started that move, had his best first-team game for us at left-back. It is very satisfying to see someone like Gary progress through the ranks at Anfield from apprentice; and being Liverpool-born it means that fans who know Gary, know his family or know somebody who does, will identify with him.

Underlining what an all-round display the lads gave – and not to be outdone – was Bruce Grobbelaar's superb second-half save from Paul Stewart's header. We were 2-0 ahead by then, and I don't think it affected the outcome, but the save was as important for Bruce's professional pride as anything else. After Craig's goal had put us three up our victory was crowned five minutes from the end when Barnesie linked with Peter Beardsley before striking our fourth goal and his fourteenth of the season.

It was our seventh straight away win, which speaks volumes for the players, and the tenth occasion on which they have hit four goals in a match. But while the forward players understandably attract the glare of publicity, Bruce and his defenders deserve equal credit. This was our twenty-fourth clean sheet of the season, and we have conceded only one goal in our last fifteen games, and have so far not let in any in the FA Cup.

Monday, 14 March: The semi-final draw, in which the club will be trying to clinch our twenty-first Wembley appearance since 1974, paired us with Nottingham Forest at Hillsborough. Forest are the only First Division side we have not yet played this season and we are certainly going to know each other next month because the semi-final will be sandwiched between our two League games, making three meetings in eleven days. The popular feeling appeared to be that this match would have been perfect for the final itself. But you accept what you get and we now have to hope that we play well enough on the day to ensure that we go through to meet Luton or Wimbledon on 14 May.

But first things first: we have a League game at Derby on Wednesday and that is the most important match at the moment simply because it is the next one.

Wednesday, 16 March: It was a night of mixed feelings for us. Our 1-1 draw in the rearranged fixture at the Baseball Ground means that we have equalled Leeds United's record of twenty-nine First Division games unbeaten from the start of a season. That is an achievement in itself and, indeed, by comparison we come out ahead of Leeds on points gained during the respective runs – both under the old two-points-for-a-win system and the present three-points system.

However, as we have consistently said, we are pursuing bigger prizes than an entry in the history books and there was no mood of celebration in our dressing-room. That was because the professionalism of the lads had been wounded by losing the lead we had been given by Craig Johnston's goal 10

DERBY COUNTY	LIVERPOOL
First Division	**Baseball Ground**
16 March	**26,356**
DERBY 1 (Forsyth)	
LIVERPOOL 1 (Johnston)	
DERBY	**LIVERPOOL**
Shilton	Grobbelaar
Blades	Gillespie
Forsyth	Ablett
Williams	Nicol
Wright	Spackman
Hindmarch	Hansen
McMinn	Beardsley
Lewis	Johnston
Gee	Houghton
Gregory	Barnes
Callaghan	McMahon
SUBSTITUTES:	
Garner	MacDonald
Micklewhite	Molby

▶*Peter Beardsley and Derby's Mark Wright tussling for possession in our 1-1 draw at the Baseball Ground, a result which brought us level with the Leeds United record of 29 First Division matches unbeaten from the start of a season. Derby's goalscorer Michael Forsyth looks on.*

minutes into the second half. Michael Forsyth equalized for Derby five minutes from the end and our players were disappointed about conceding only their second goal in sixteen games stretching back to December. What made it an even more frustrating night was that we were in control of the game for long periods and could have won it.

Our team was unchanged but we lost Steve McMahon just after the interval with an ankle injury sustained in the first half – and that gave Jan Molby the chance of making only his second appearance of the season. Also on the bench tonight was Kevin MacDonald, a significant step for him. It was the first time he has been included in the thirteen since breaking his left leg at Southampton back in September 1986.

There was a tremendous atmosphere at Derby tonight generated by a 26,000-plus crowd just a few hundred short of capacity and the biggest League attendance at the Baseball Ground for eight years. It means that we have attracted the biggest crowds of the season at twelve of our fifteen away games so far – the exceptions being the live TV games at Manchester United and Newcastle and our December fixture at Southampton. If public response is a yardstick of the quality of football our lads are producing then they are passing with flying colours.

Thursday, 17 March: An eventful FA Youth Cup quarter-final at Anfield ended with our youngsters drawing 3-3 with Nottingham Forest and facing a replay at the City Ground next Thursday. Goals from Brian McGorry, skipper Charlie Boyd and Craig Hignett put us 3-0 up after an hour but Forest fought back to level through Tony Abrahams, Alan Lamb and Lee Glover.

Sunday, 20 March: The media concentration on making comparisons between the Leeds United team of 1974 and ours reached epidemic proportions before today's 138th League derby meeting with Everton which we lost 1-0. I said before

EVERTON	LIVERPOOL
First Division	**Goodison Park**
20 March	**44,162**

EVERTON 1 (Clarke)
LIVERPOOL 0

EVERTON	LIVERPOOL
Southall	Grobbelaar
Stevens	Gillespie
Pointon	Ablett
Van Den Hauwe	Nicol
Watson	Spackman
Reid	Hansen
Steven	Beardsley
Clarke	Johnston
Sharp	Houghton
Harper	Barnes
Sheedy	McMahon

SUBSTITUTES:	
Heath	Watson
Power	Molby

◄ *The goal that ended our unbeaten League run: the ball evades a ruck of players following an Everton corner and Wayne Clarke scores.*

►*England colleagues on opposite sides in the heat of a Mersey derby as John Barnes duels with Everton's Trevor Steven.*

the game – as I have repeated through the season – that setting records was in no way our main priority. I also stressed that whatever the qualities of Billy Bremner, Johnny Giles and company, they were not going to be playing against us today. Our task was to try to beat Everton – and we failed to do it because we did not transform our control of the game into chances and goals.

We are disappointed about the result not because we have missed an entry in the record books but because we have lost three points. If we had won or drawn it would not only have established an unprecedented sequence of thirty First Division games unbeaten from the start of a season but also equalled Burnley's record of thirty matches undefeated during a season set in 1920-21. But our big regret is that we failed to secure more points towards our attempt to win the championship and I suppose that sharing Everton's joy in beating us for the second time this season – following their Littlewoods Cup win – will be the bookmakers who apparently stood to lose £1 million if we had completed the League programme unbeaten. I have never seen a poor bookie and pardon me if I don't share their relief over the result! Apart from being our first League defeat in thirty-two outings stretching back to Coventry last May and our first of any kind in twenty-five games since Everton knocked us out of the Littlewoods Cup in October we have collected a crop of injuries.

The goal that won the game for Everton came in the 15th minute from Wayne Clarke, whose brother Allan, a member of the Leeds team of 1974, was watching from the Press Box where he was working as a radio contributor. We had more possession than Everton but we did not make it count and that is nobody's fault but our own.

Liverpool's sequence of 29 First Division games unbeaten from the start of the season until their 1-0 defeat at Everton on Sunday, 20 March, 1988 equalled the record set by Leeds United in 1973-74. The respective statistics are:

	P	W	D	L	F	A	Pts
Leeds	29	19	10	0	51	16	48

(67 under present system)

	P	W	D	L	F	A	Pts
Liverpool	29	22	7	0	67	13	73

(51 under old system)

Monday, 21 March: The immediate legacy of yesterday's match is that Steve McMahon, who suffered more ankle damage, has had to withdraw from the England squad for Wednesday's international against Holland at Wembley. That is a big personal blow for Steve, who impressed on his international debut in Israel last month. But the condition of his ankle after a check-up today ruled out any hope of his joining Bobby Robson's squad.

Gary Gillespie and Steve Nicol, also casualties of the Everton game, have had to withdraw from Scotland's squad to meet Malta tomorrow and Ray Houghton's thigh injury means that he has to miss the Republic of Ireland's game against Rumania along with John Aldridge and Ronnie Whelan.

Thursday, 24 March: The news reached the Press that Mark Lawrenson's playing career is over because of Achilles tendon damage and that he is to leave Anfield to take over as manager of Oxford United. Our club was still engaged in sorting out the formalities involved with insurance over Mark and would have preferred the announcement of his enforced playing retirement to have been delayed. Obviously within the club we had known for a little while that Mark was not going to play again. It was a medical decision both he and we have got to accept but for a player of his calibre at thirty years old it is a personal disaster.

Mark had several years left of his career at Liverpool and he had been looking forward to the prospect of playing for the Republic of Ireland in this summer's European Championships in West Germany. He has been a tremendous performer for Liverpool since he joined us for the club's then record fee of £900,000 from Brighton in 1981. We were neighbours in Southport and we have enjoyed a great deal of success together with Liverpool in domestic and European football.

Mark's Achilles problem dates back to a moment two minutes before the interval in our home First Division game with Wimbledon on 28 March last year. He was moving with the ball at his feet and suddenly pulled up – his Achilles band had snapped. There was nobody else involved. Clearly, it was a bad injury and Mark was taken to hospital and operated on that same day. Needless to say, he had the best of medical supervision and also spells at the FA's National Rehabilitation Centre before returning to first-team action – ahead of expectations – as a substitute in our home game with Charlton in September.

Ironically, an Achilles injury to Barry Venison in October

presented Mark with his chance for a run in the first team spanning nine games until he limped off with hamstring trouble at Southampton in December. He was back in the team for the two matches against Stoke that launched our FA Cup campaign but in the next game against Arsenal he limped off again after suffering another Achilles setback. That was Mark's last appearance for us and I am sure he will be the first to agree that since his operation last season he has not been the same player. There was an obvious loss of power in his leg.

Mark must be one of the best players ever to have worn a Liverpool jersey. He was a great tackler, with tremendous pace and powers of recovery, and formed a marvellous central defensive partnership with Alan Hansen. But in addition to those qualities Mark also possessed unselfish versatility by filling every back-four position and also operating in midfield. He was prepared to play anywhere he was asked and the importance of players like this to a squad cannot be overstated. Mark has been a cornerstone of Liverpool Football Club and a major contributor to its success.

It is a tragedy for him and a blow for us that his playing career has ended so prematurely. But he has to look to the future now. He was given permission by Liverpool to discuss other offers in the game. On the positive side is the fact that Mark has been fortunate to find another job so quickly, especially in the First Division at managerial level. We wish him all the best – except if his Oxford team happen to play us!

While Mark's fate was breaking to the media tonight, our youth team went down 3-0 at Nottingham Forest in their FA Youth Cup quarter-final replay. Naturally, we are disappointed for John Bennison, Malcolm Cook and their lads. But they have done tremendously well to reach this stage and their progress has shown the promise of these youngsters.

Saturday, 26 March: The prompt action of Bobby Robson and his England staff ensured that Peter Beardsley was able to play today in our 2-1 home win over Wimbledon, ironically the opposition when Mark Lawrenson was injured a year ago. Peter took a kick on the knee during England's 2-2 draw with Holland at Wembley on Wednesday and he was immediately substituted, so reducing the risk of the damage worsening. I am grateful to Bobby and when he telephoned me to inquire how Peter was I thanked him for his thoughtfulness and co-operation. This is a perfect example of what relationships between club and country should be like.

LIVERPOOL	WIMBLEDON
First Division	**Anfield**
26 March	**36,464**

LIVERPOOL 2 (Aldridge, Barnes)

WIMBLEDON 1 (Young)

LIVERPOOL	WIMBLEDON
Grobbelaar	Beasant
Gillespie	Scales
Ablett	Phelan
Nicol	Ryan
Spackman	Young
Hansen	Thorn
Beardsley	Cunningham
Aldridge	Cork
Johnston	Fashanu
Barnes	Sanchez
McMahon	Wise

SUBSTITUTES:

Dalglish	Sayer
Molby	Clement

◀▲ *A handshake for John Aldridge as I come on as substitute for him in the 87th minute of our home win over Wimbledon which gave me a chance to stretch my legs and exercise my vocal chords!*

It allowed Peter to line up against Wimbledon but we were without Ray Houghton, after his thigh injury in last Sunday's derby game, and Steve McMahon struggled and failed to complete the match because of his ankle problem. However, we did have John Aldridge back after missing four matches with a thigh injury and he emphasized his finishing skills by putting us in front with a magnificent 34th-minute header past Dave Beasant from Steve Nicol's cross. It was his twenty-

▲ *Not many people look down on lanky 'Jocky' Hansen but Wimbledon's goalkeeping captain Dave Beasant, all 6ft 4in of him, is one of them. The two skippers are pictured, with referee George Courtney and his linesmen, before our home League game.*

second goal of the season, underlining what a valuable contribution he has made. However sweet a team's build-up might be you always need somebody on the end of things to put the ball in the net – and that is John's strength.

After Jan Molby had replaced Steve McMahon in the 72nd minute – Jan's first home appearance of the season – John Barnes put us 2-0 ahead with his fifteenth goal of the season and his 100th at club level for us and Watford. But our fellow FA Cup semi-finalists Wimbledon are never a team to lie down. They play forcefully to their strengths in their own style and they are not unhappy when the ball is in the air. And it was from an aerial challenge that they cut our lead in the 89th minute when Eric Young went up to head in a left-wing corner from Dennis Wise. It was the first home goal we have conceded since the Chelsea game on 6 December and only the second at Anfield in the League since the thrilling duel with Charlton in September.

I had gone on as substitute for John Aldridge just before the goal to avoid the chance of him suffering a late injury setback after missing four games. What a tactical stroke that was! The opposition scored just after my entrance for my first taste of senior football this season and I twice ended up at the corner flag trying to keep possession and protect our lead through injury time. But we won and that was a nice feeling after our disappointment at Everton. This was our first match at Anfield for seven weeks and one of only nine Saturday home games all season. That amazingly low total is due to games being switched to Sundays, blank weekends caused by the First Division reduction process and the early-season closure of the Kop.

I appreciate, as our chief executive Peter Robinson has said publicly, that this can cause the club cash-flow problems. But from a playing viewpoint my attitude is that we have twenty home League games and twenty away and we just have to get on with playing them in whatever order they come and on whatever days they are played. And in cup competitions you have to accept what you are given by the luck – or otherwise – of the draw and just be satisfied that you are still involved. My only exception to that is when teams are drawn away at clubs with plastic pitches. As I have said before, that goes beyond the luck of the draw.

I do think, however, that playing games on Sundays has taken some adjusting to by everyone in football, spectators included. Even now I detect a slightly nore subdued crowd reaction during Sunday matches compared to Saturday games and perhaps that is only to be expected because it has changed the habits of many people's lives. Clearly, though, as long as the television authorities feel it is a good day for screening games, Sunday football is here to stay.

Monday, 28 March: After my brief appearance at Anfield on Saturday, I tasted a bit more action tonight when I turned out for a Tottenham XI against Manchester United at White Hart Lane in a testimonial game for Danny Thomas. Steve Hodge and Steve Archibald scored for our side but two goals from Gordon Strachan and another from Peter Davenport gave United a 3-2 win in front of a crowd of more than 20,000.

Wednesday, 30 March: Barry Venison returned to action in the reserves tonight following his appendix operation; and he was on the winning side with a 4-0 victory over Blackpool. It was a happy night for our reserve striker John Durnin who scored twice after signing a new two-year contract.

It was also announced today that our captain Alan Hansen is to have a plum testimonial against an England team chosen by Bobby Robson to be staged at Anfield on Monday, 9 May. Liverpool v England – that is a mouth-watering fixture and as Alan will be picking our team that night I'd better speak nicely to him!

▲ *A new strip for a night. I wore this Tottenham gear as a guest player in Danny Thomas's Testimonial match against Manchester United at White Hart Lane.*

DIVISION ONE

	P	Home					Away					Pts
		W	D	L	F	A	W	D	L	F	A	
Liverpool	31	13	2	0	38	4	10	5	1	31	11	76
Man Utd	33	9	5	1	26	13	8	6	4	25	18	62
Everton	32	13	2	1	28	5	4	6	6	16	14	59
QPR	32	11	3	4	27	13	5	4	5	12	19	55
Nottm For	30	7	4	2	28	11	8	5	4	25	16	54
Arsenal	31	10	3	4	32	14	5	5	4	14	14	53
Wimbledon	31	8	6	2	26	13	5	3	7	20	21	48
Tottenham	35	8	5	5	24	21	3	5	9	11	21	43
Sheff Wed	33	9	1	7	21	21	4	3	9	18	32	43
Southmptn	33	4	6	6	18	20	6	4	7	21	24	40
Coventry	32	4	6	5	20	23	6	4	7	19	25	40
Newcastle	31	5	5	5	19	20	4	7	5	19	24	39
Norwich	33	6	3	7	22	23	5	3	9	12	20	39
Luton	28	8	4	3	29	15	3	1	9	11	23	38
West Ham	32	5	7	4	18	18	3	5	8	14	25	36
Derby	32	4	6	6	14	14	4	5	7	14	20	35
Chelsea	33	6	7	2	19	13	2	3	13	23	45	34
Charlton	33	5	6	6	19	20	2	5	9	13	27	32
Portsmth	31	4	7	6	18	22	2	5	7	9	26	30
Oxford	31	5	4	6	23	28	1	6	9	16	34	28
Watford	31	3	3	10	10	21	2	5	8	9	20	23

APRIL

Saturday, 2 April, 1988: The first of our three-match series with Nottingham Forest over the course of eleven days ended in disappointment for us today when we went down 2-1 at the City Ground. It was only our second League defeat of the season but it was a match in which we hardly got a break of luck.

The after-match questions from the media centred on my team selection rather than the game. Jan Molby, who has had wretched fortune with injuries, started a senior game for the first time this season. He came into a five-man midfield, with John Aldridge operating as central striker serviced from the flanks by Craig Johnston and John Barnes. I named Peter Beardsley as a substitute along with Ray Houghton, who had recovered from the thigh injury that kept him out of last week's game against Wimbledon. It is not my policy to discuss the reasons for my team selection in public and I do not intend to start now. The team I picked was chosen in the best interests of Liverpool FC and it is a formation I believe we can operate well. Certainly it is one I will use again in the future if and when I think it is necessary.

▼ *An agonizing moment in the League match at Nottingham Forest as the ball deflects off Alan Hansen and into our net to give Forest the lead.*

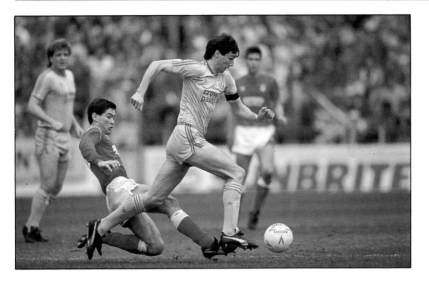

◀ *Alan Hansen sweeps past Nigel Clough during our League match at Nottingham Forest.*

◀ *Forest's Gary Crosby goes down under challenge from Gary Gillespie.*

NOTTINGHAM FOREST	LIVERPOOL

First Division	City Ground
2 April	29,188

NOTTINGHAM 2 (Hansen o.g., Clough)

LIVERPOOL 1 (Aldridge pen)

NOTTINGHAM	LIVERPOOL
Sutton	Grobbelaar
Chettle	Gillespie
Pearce	Ablett
Walker	Nicol
Foster	Spackman
Wilson	Hansen
Crosby	Molby
Webb	Aldridge
Clough	Johnston
Wilkinson	Barnes
Rice	McMahon

SUBSTITUTES:

Glover	Beardsley
Carr	Houghton

I said earlier that we hardly got a break during the match. The only one we did get was provided by Bruce Grobbelaar, who dived to his left to save Nigel Clough's 46th-minute penalty, awarded for Gary Gillespie's challenge on Gary Crosby, Forest's tricky little winger. By then we were trailing to a first-half own goal by Alan Hansen. But there was nothing Alan could have done about it as Neil Webb's cross went off him and past Bruce into the net.

We had just brought on Peter Beardsley to replace Jan Molby when Forest went 2-0 up after 59 minutes, Nigel Clough scoring from a pull-back by Crosby. Our lads kept plugging away and we cut the deficit when John Aldridge scored his twenty-third goal of the season from the penalty spot after Webb had fouled John Barnes. In the remaining 20 minutes we might have got something out of the game. However, it was not to be. But it was not a wasted afternoon. We learned a lot about Forest from our first meeting with them this season . . . but left them wondering a bit about us.

LIVERPOOL	MANCHESTER UNITED

First Division   Anfield

4 April   43,497

LIVERPOOL 3 (Beardsley, Gillespie, McMahon)

MAN UNITED 3 (Robson 2, Strachan)

LIVERPOOL	MAN UNITED
Grobbelaar	Turner
Gillespie	Anderson
Ablett	Blackmore
Nicol	Bruce
Spackman	McGrath
Hansen	Duxbury
Beardsley	Robson
Aldridge	Strachan
Houghton	McClair
Barnes	Davenport
McMahon	Gibson

SUBSTITUTES:

Johnston	Whiteside
Dalglish	Olsen

Easter Monday, 4 April: The crowd of more than 43,000 certainly had their money's worth from today's pulsating 3-3 draw with Manchester United at Anfield. I brought Peter Beardsley and Ray Houghton back into the starting line-up, with Craig Johnston and Jan Molby dropping out, Craig sitting alongside me on the substitutes' bench.

The match was not three minutes old when United scored, Bryan Robson applying the finish to Peter Davenport's pass. It was a good goal from United's viewpoint but a bad one from ours because we set it up by losing possession. But from then on we assumed command of the game and played some lovely football, completely dominating United. Our reward was a 38th-minute equalizer by Peter Beardsley, after Ray Houghton's cross beat Steve Bruce, and a goal to put us in front three minutes later. This time Peter acted as a supplier by crossing from the right for John Barnes to put the ball back in from the left and Gary Gillespie to head it powerfully into the Kop net. We increased our lead with one of the goals of the season a minute after the interval, when Steve McMahon ran through a tackle by Mike Duxbury to score with a scorching twenty-yard shot past Chris Turner.

But any thoughts we had of claiming only our second League win over United in seventeen meetings were to be dispelled in dramatic fashion. United sent on substitutes Norman Whiteside and Jesper Olsen in the 54th minute to replace Clayton Blackmore and Duxbury – and five minutes later they were reduced to ten men when Colin Gibson, earlier cautioned for dissent, was sent off by referee John Key after tripping Steve Nicol. But United, to their credit, showed fighting spirit even if Whiteside again upset our fans and was booked for fouling Steve McMahon. Norman would not win a popularity poll on the Kop, but that's the way he is.

United had that crucial break of fortune on their side in the

▶ *Craig Johnston and Manchester United's Paul McGrath in a tussle during the 3-3 draw at Anfield.*

66th minute when Robson's shot deflected off Gary Gillespie and into the net with Bruce Grobbelaar wrong-footed. We could have scored again but John Aldridge had two good efforts kept out, one by Bruce and one by Turner, before United crowned their ten-man campaign when Davenport's pass sent Gordon Strachan through for their equalizing goal. It was disappointing for us to lose a 3-1 lead but United can justifiably feel pleased with themselves. They have been unbeaten on their last eight League visits to Anfield, winning four and drawing four. But at the end of the day I am sure they would swap that record against us for the overall success Liverpool have enjoyed.

Prominent in the media reports of an entertaining holiday game was my after-match disagreement with United manager Alex Ferguson, who said in a radio interview that he felt Anfield intimidated referees into making certain decisions. I was in the Anfield corridor carrying our new baby daughter Lauren when I heard Alex voicing that claim. So I said to the interviewer: 'You might as well talk to my daughter . . . you'll get more sense out of her.' But I can quash rumours here and now that a certain newspaper wanted to do a signed-article with Lauren!

Seriously, though, I have no wish to have a slanging match with anybody. But when you feel something has been said or done that threatens the best interests of Liverpool FC you have to respond and that is why I said what I did.

Saturday, 9 April: Our lads did us proud at Hillsborough today when they beat Forest 2-1 in the FA Cup semi-final to book the club's twenty-first Wembley appearance since 1974 – a meeting with Wimbledon, who beat Luton in the other semi, in the Final on 14 May.

John Barnes, who had breathing difficulties after being elbowed in last Monday's game against United, recovered to take his place in an unchanged team and make a massive contribution to our success. A run by him in the 13th minute proved unlucky for Forest. Barnesie was chopped down by Steve Chettle and John Aldridge did his customary efficient job from the penalty spot to beat Steve Sutton and put us in front. But John is an admirable finisher as well as master penalty-taker, and he displayed this for our second goal in the 52nd minute. Peter Beardsley linked with John Barnes on the left – a combination that has been very significant in our Cup run – and when Barnesie put the cross in John Aldridge met it on the volley to leave Sutton helpless.

Forest got back in the game in the 67th minute when Nigel

LIVERPOOL	NOTTINGHAM FOREST

FA Cup Hillsborough

9 April 51,627

LIVERPOOL 2 (Aldridge 2 inc. 1 pen)

NOTTINGHAM 1 (Clough)

LIVERPOOL	NOTTINGHAM
Grobbelaar	Sutton
Gillespie	Chettle
Ablett	Pearce
Nicol	Walker
Spackman	Foster
Hansen	Wilson
Beardsley	Crosby
Aldridge	Webb
Houghton	Clough
Barnes	Wilkinson
McMahon	Rice

SUBSTITUTES:

Johnston	Glover
Molby	Fleming

▶ *A jubilant moment as I celebrate with our supporters following our FA Cup semi-final victory over Nottingham Forest at Hillsborough.*

▲ *John Aldridge receives the congratulations of Nigel Spackman and Gary Ablett after scoring our second goal in the 2-1 FA Cup semi-final win over Nottingham Forest.*

Clough scored, but we had the chances to win by a bigger margin and I do not think anybody can dispute that we were the better side and deserved the result. Forest manager Brian Clough said as much on television afterwards.

Sunday, 10 April: While we believe at Anfield that the team as a unit is the most important factor in the quest for success, we are always delighted about individual recognition for the players. Both these things were celebrated at tonight's Professional Footballers Association Awards dinner.

John Barnes was voted Player of the Year, Steve McMahon was second in the poll, Peter Beardsley third and our skipper Alan Hansen also in the short list of six contenders chosen by their fellow professionals. It is a great tribute to Barnesie, who has done his own thing in the framework of the Liverpool team. He has been prepared to make sacrifices to help the side. It is also a compliment to the rest of the squad at Anfield that they have fitted in with his style.

▶ *John Barnes receives the PFA Award as Player of the Year from England manager Bobby Robson.*

Wednesday, 13 April: If our performance against Forest in the semi-final at Hillsborough last Saturday was impressive, our display in beating them 5-0 in tonight's League game at Anfield was magnificent. Tom Finney, one of the greatest figures in the history of British football and one of its best players, was a guest at Anfield tonight and said he had not seen our performance bettered by any side, including Brazilians. Certainly it was a great exhibition of football; but perhaps the fact that this was the latest one dims the memory slightly about other fine performances our team has produced this season.

The lads produced such variation tonight. Movement, passing, finishing – it was all there in abundance. I think our lads were so good that the result does not reflect badly on any Forest player. Indeed, their goalkeeper Steve Sutton kept the score down by producing several outstanding saves. The move that put us ahead in the 18th minute was launched at the back by Alan Hansen, whose pass sent Ray Houghton through to exchange passes with John Barnes and score his seventh goal of the season in brilliant style. Our goalkeeper Bruce Grobbelaar emphasized his understated importance to us by making a very good save from Nigel Clough when the score was still only 1-0.

However, we increased our lead in the 37th minute when John Aldridge put away a marvellous long pass from Peter Beardsley, and we made it three in the 57th minute with Gary Gillespie volleying into the roof of the Kop net from Ray Houghton's low cross. Peter Beardsley scored our fourth in the 78th minute after Barnesie had cut in from the left. We made two substitutions after that – Jan Molby and Craig Johnston replacing Steve McMahon and Ray Houghton respectively. Yet the lads kept their football going to the last second and were rewarded with a fifth goal two minutes from the end when Peter Beardsley and Nigel Spackman combined for John Aldridge to score his twenty-seventh goal of the season – and his fifth in our three-match series with Forest.

Looking back on the games, if we'd had to choose one to lose it would have been a League match because at least we could afford to.

Friday, 15 April: Our departure for Wembley today to take part in tomorrow's League Centenary Festival was preceded by some disappointing news. Barry Venison, who was just getting over an appendix operation in March, has undergone Achilles tendon surgery.

Also ruled out of the Wembley weekend are Jan Molby and

▲ *The goalkeeper who lost his head! Bruce Grobbelaar gives the fans a laugh during our 5-0 First Division victory over Nottingham Forest at Anfield.*

LIVERPOOL	NOTTINGHAM FOREST

First Division	**Anfield**
13 April	**39,535**

LIVERPOOL 5 (Houghton, Aldridge 2, Gillespie, Beardsley)

NOTTINGHAM 0

LIVERPOOL	NOTTINGHAM
Grobbelaar	Sutton
Gillespie	Chettle
Ablett	Pearce
Nicol	Walker
Spackman	Foster
Hansen	Wilson
Beardsley	Crosby
Aldridge	Webb
Houghton	Clough
Barnes	Glover
McMahon	Rice

SUBSTITUTES:	
Molby	Gaynor
Johnston	Wassall

LIVERPOOL	NEWCASTLE UNITED

Mercantile Credit Centenary Festival — **Wembley**

16 April

LIVERPOOL 0

NEWCASTLE 0 (Newcastle won 1-0 on penalty scored by McDonald)

LIVERPOOL	NEWCASTLE
Hooper	Kelly
Gillespie	McDonald
Ablett	Anderson
Nicol	McCreery
Watson	Tinnion
MacDonald	Roeder
Staunton	Gascoigne
Aldridge	O'Neill
Johnston	Wharton
Barnes	Mirandinha
McMahon	Goddard

SUBSTITUTES:

Beardsley	Stephenson
Durnin	

▶ *John Barnes goes off with a groin injury near the end of our Football League Centenary Festival game against Newcastle at Wembley.*

Nigel Spackman, who both have calf injuries, and Ray Houghton, who has a thigh problem. Their absences are, of course, in addition to those of Ronnie Whelan and Jim Beglin, who are still awaiting comeback games.

Saturday, 16 April: The action started early at Wembley this morning. We kicked off at 10.50am in our Festival match against Newcastle and after 20 minutes each way it was still 0-0. So that meant a sudden-death penalty decider with Newcastle going through after Gary Kelly, who had played well throughout, saved Steve McMahon's spot kick and Neil McDonald scored with his penalty against Mike Hooper.

However, we should have won the game without resort to sudden death and I was as disappointed with our result as I was pleased with our performance. But the main worry centred on John Barnes who had to limp off with groin damage just two minutes from the end of the match, making him doubtful for Wednesday's game at Norwich.

Sunday, 17 April: Our Fourth Division neighbours Tranmere, the Birkenhead club on the other side of the Mersey who have had their problems in recent years, have really done themselves proud. After beating Wimbledon and Newcastle yesterday, they went out to Nottingham Forest in today's Festival semi-final only on penalties after a 2-2 draw and their exploits on the field as well as the number of supporters they had at Wembley reflects great credit on the club.

Wednesday, 20 April: Norwich City tonight completed a unique double of their own. They became the first team to prevent us scoring in two League meetings this season – and at the same time kept us waiting in our attempt to clinch the championship. Our goalless draw at Carrow Road was a repeat of the scoreline at Anfield in November and instrumental in that, just as he was in front of the Kop, was Norwich goalkeeper Bryan Gunn.

As we feared, John Barnes was ruled out because of his groin injury and we played Craig Johnston wide on the left flank. It was the first time we have been without Barnesie this season but we still could have won the game. The result means that we need one more point before we can call ourselves champions and although some people remarked that the champagne remained on ice there was none ever in our dressing-room. Mind you, if we had won we might have bought some!

Nottingham Forest's draw with West Ham tonight ended their title challenge, which means that Manchester United are now our sole rivals. To pip us they will have to win their last four games and rely on us losing our last five. They would also have to turn around our goal difference advantage of thirty-two.

NORWICH CITY	LIVERPOOL
First Division	Carrow Road
20 April	22,509
NORWICH 0	
LIVERPOOL 0	
NORWICH	**LIVERPOOL**
Gunn	Grobbelaar
Culverhouse	Gillespie
Spearing	Ablett
Linighan	Nicol
Phelan	Spackman
Butterworth	Hansen
Fox	Beardsley
Drinkell	Aldridge
Fleck	Houghton
Goss	Johnston
Putney	McMahon
SUBSTITUTES:	
Rosario	MacDonald
Gordon	Staunton

◀ *Ray Houghton cannot believe his bad luck after a near miss in our goalless draw at Norwich.*

Thursday, 21 April: Although our reserve team had a disappointing result tonight by losing 2-0 at Nottingham Forest – which is a setback to their hopes of bringing another Central League title to Anfield – the match did have a big plus for us. Ronnie Whelan, who had not had a game of any kind since damaging his knee in January and subsequently undergoing micro-surgery, returned to action and played for 75 minutes without suffering any reaction. That is great news because the more players we have in contention the better.

Saturday, 23 April: The lads have done it! Our 1-0 win over Tottenham this afternoon secured us the championship and it is a marvellous feeling. No matter how many times you experience the thrill of winning the title – and I am fortunate enough to have been involved in seven since I signed for Liverpool from Celtic in 1977 – that special tingle never diminishes. The last time we won it, in 1986, was my first season as player-manager when I appeared in the team frequently. This season, apart from the last three minutes against Wimbledon, I have not figured in the side at all. But having sat and watched the lads become champions I feel just as elated now as I was the last time and the time before that. It has been a triumph for the whole squad and the emphasis we place on collective involvement.

To win the championship still with four games left – which is twelve points at stake – is to the credit of every single player and, not least, to my very capable right-hand men Ronnie Moran and Roy Evans whose assistance, knowledge and expertise cannot be exaggerated. They have been invaluable to me ever since I became manager in 1985, but this season,

▼ *The Kop salute our championship triumph after the match against Tottenham which we won 1-0.*

my first since Bob Paisley's agreed spell as managerial consultant expired, their help and co-operation have assumed even greater importance.

Seven members of our squad – today's match winner Peter Beardsley, John Barnes (who had to miss today's game with continued groin problems and also withdraw from England's trip to Hungary), John Aldridge, Barry Venison, Nigel Spackman, Ray Houghton and Gary Ablett – are sampling the joy of winning their first championship medals. Now they have got the taste I am sure they will want more. It can only encourage them. They have won their first one in style.

Because it is a first time for so many in the squad, some of the pundits have labelled this *my* team. I refute that. It is not my team any more than the first team selection I made in the summer of 1985. It is Liverpool's team and I am only a

LIVERPOOL	TOTTENHAM HOTSPUR
First Division	**Anfield**
23 April	**44,798**

LIVERPOOL 1 (Beardsley)
TOTTENHAM 0

LIVERPOOL	TOTTENHAM
Grobbelaar	Mimms
Gillespie	Statham
Ablett	Thomas
Nicol	Metgod
Spackman	Fairclough
Hansen	Mabbutt
Beardsley	Walsh
Aldridge	P. Allen
Houghton	Waddle
Johnston	Samways
McMahon	Hodge

SUBSTITUTES:

Dalglish	C. Allen
MacDonald	Ruddock

◀ *Our squad, whose superb performances brought the club its seventeenth League championship.*

◀ *The championship is won and the paper cups are out in the dressing-room to quaff some bubbly after the title-clinching win over Tottenham. With me left to right are Ronnie Moran, Roy Evans and Tom Saunders.*

▲ *Looks like I've won another cap! One of many lighthearted moments during the recording of 'Anfield Rap', written by Craig Johnston and performed by the lads in great style.*

caretaker. From the moment I took on the job I was prepared to stand or fall by the team's success or failure. This club has awesome standards to maintain, even to better, and that is the task I am charged with. This is the club's seventeenth League championship and the ninth in thirteen seasons but we are always looking for the next one.

Having said that, whatever happens against Wimbledon at Wembley in the FA Cup Final, I have enjoyed this season. We lost Ian Rush to Italy and the lads who came in have done their stuff brilliantly. Congratulations to everyone. And I will tell you one thing for sure . . . the champagne certainly flowed tonight!

Saturday, 30 April: Before today's game at Stamford Bridge it was announced that John Barnes had been voted Footballer of the Year by members of the Football Writers Association, with Alan Hansen runner-up. Following his similar accolade from his fellow players of the Professional Footballers Association it is another tremendous tribute to John, and our squad in general, that he has completed the 'double'. Apparently, John collected two-thirds of the votes of the nation's soccer writers and Liverpool players polled ninety-six per cent of the total. I am just racking my brains wondering who the other four per cent went to!

John is due to be presented with the award at London's Royal Lancaster Hotel on Thursday, 12 May – two days before we meet Wimbledon in the FA Cup Final. There was no doubt that John celebrated today's announcement in style, with a magnificent equalizer at Chelsea this afternoon.

I made a few team changes from last week's title-clinching game against Tottenham because, with Wembley looming, it was an ideal opportunity to give some players a taste of first-team action and to rest others. Among the lads I rested was Gary Gillespie who continued our squad's productive season off the field when he and his wife Susan this week celebrated the arrival of twin daughters Ruth and Rachel. This double addition to the Gillespie household follows the recent arrivals in the Dalglish and Grobbelaar families. There must be something in the Anfield air!

Alex Watson came in for his second senior appearance today at centre-back and, just like his performance at QPR on his debut in March, he was again impressive in a disappointing 1-1 draw. Ronnie Whelan also had a valuable senior outing at left-back, with Gary Ablett on the substitutes' bench alongside Peter Beardsley. But shortly after Peter had replaced John Aldridge in the 69th minute,

◀ *This Steve Nicol tussle with Kerry Dixon gave Chelsea the penalty from which Gordon Durie scored during the 1-1 draw at Stamford Bridge.*

Chelsea were awarded a penalty for Steve Nicol holding back Kerry Dixon. Gordon Durie took the spot kick and scored.

Three minutes later, though, we equalized in spectacular fashion through Barnesie, who crowned his FWA award and his return to the team after groin trouble by providing a marvellous memory of a disappointing match. He was fouled thirty yards out and after Nigel Spackman – playing against his former club – ran over the ball Barnesie curled the free kick left-footed into the top corner of the net. It was his sixteenth goal of the season and one of the best.

We could have won the game four minutes from the end when we got a penalty after Ray Houghton had been brought down. With our regular penalty-taker John Aldridge off the field, Peter Beardsley took the kick. Chelsea goalkeeper Kevin Hitchcock, who had seen Peter take a spot kick in our FA Cup tie at Maine Road in March before his move to Stamford Bridge from Mansfield, guessed right and saved the penalty to ensure that the game ended 1-1.

CHELSEA	LIVERPOOL

First Division	Stamford Bridge
30 April	**35,265**

CHELSEA 1 (Durie pen)

LIVERPOOL 1 (Barnes)

CHELSEA	LIVERPOOL
Hitchcock	Grobbelaar
Hall	Watson
Dorigo	Whelan
Wicks	Nicol
McLaughlin	Spackman
Clarke	Hansen
Nevin	Johnston
Hazard	Aldridge
Dixon	Houghton
Durie	Barnes
Bumstead	McMahon

SUBSTITUTES:	
West	Beardsley
Pates	Ablett

▲ *A gem from John Barnes as he smashes a free kick past Chelsea's 'wall' and goalkeeper Kevin Hitchcock.*

DIVISION ONE

	P	Home W	D	L	F	A	Away W	D	L	F	A	Pts
Liverpool	**37**	**15**	**3**	**0**	**47**	**7**	**10**	**7**	**2**	**33**	**14**	**85**
Man Utd........	37	12	5	1	35	15	8	7	4	28	21	72
Everton	38	14	4	1	33	9	5	8	6	19	16	69
QPR..............	39	12	4	4	30	14	7	5	7	18	24	66
Nottm For	36	9	6	2	32	13	9	5	5	26	21	65
Arsenal	38	11	3	5	34	15	6	8	5	21	22	62
Wimbledon...	37	8	8	3	31	19	5	6	7	24	25	53
Sheff Wed.....	38	10	2	7	26	25	5	5	9	24	35	52
Coventry.......	38	6	7	6	23	25	7	5	7	22	27	51
Newcastle.....	38	8	6	5	30	22	4	8	7	21	29	50
Southmptn...	38	6	7	6	26	25	6	5	8	21	26	48
Luton	34	10	5	3	37	19	3	2	11	13	32	46
Norwich........	38	7	5	7	26	25	5	4	10	14	24	45
Tottenham....	38	8	5	6	24	22	3	5	11	11	24	43
Derby	39	6	6	7	18	17	4	6	10	17	28	42
Chelsea.........	38	7	10	2	23	16	2	4	13	25	47	41
Charlton	38	7	6	6	22	20	2	7	10	14	30	40
West Ham	38	5	9	5	19	20	3	6	10	16	29	39
Portsmth	38	4	8	7	20	25	3	6	10	14	35	35
Watford	39	4	5	11	15	24	3	6	10	11	25	32
Oxford	38	5	7	7	24	32	1	6	12	17	41	31

MAY

Monday, 2 May, 1988: Today was coronation day – the day our players who have performed so superbly during the season finally got their hands on the championship trophy. Or, in this case, two trophies. As well as the traditional piece of silverware, we were also presented with the new Barclays trophy, from the Football League sponsors Barclays Bank, and their cheque for £50,000.

It had been arranged that the presentations – made by League secretary Graham Kelly and Barclays Bank chairman John Quinton – would take place on the pitch before today's Bank Holiday game against Southampton. But, in hindsight, it is worth considering reverting to after-match presentations if possible because I suspect that pre-match ceremonies can rob players of concentration in the game that follows. I agree with our captain Alan Hansen that after running around the ground showing off the trophies to our jubilant supporters it is very difficult to snap out of that festive mood and recapture the right attitude to play a serious, competitive match.

Our performance in today's 1-1 draw certainly bore that out. It was not the type of display we have come to expect from our players and although my disappointment might sound churlish, with the championship trophies standing in our dressing-room, the season is far from over yet. We have two more League games to come, as well as the FA Cup Final, and the public who come to watch us have a right to expect the standard of entertainment associated with Liverpool, quite apart from our desire to complete our second Double in three seasons.

Today we took the lead four minutes before half-time when John Barnes went past Gerry Forrest and crossed for John Aldridge to score his twenty-eighth goal of the season. Peter Beardsley went within a coat of paint of putting us 2-0 in front when he swept on to Ray Houghton's 62nd-minute pass, beat Derek Statham and goalkeeper John Burridge only to see his shot hit the foot of the far post. If that had gone in I think we would have won the game. But within six minutes of that incident Southampton equalized with a magnificent goal, struck right-footed by Rodney Wallace, eighteen-year-old brother of Danny, from Colin Clarke's cross. It was Rodney's second full game for Southampton's first team and he announced afterwards that he would remember his first senior goal for the rest of his life.

LIVERPOOL	SOUTHMPTN

First Division   Anfield

2 May   37,610

LIVERPOOL 1 (Aldridge)
SOUTHMPTN 1 (R. Wallace)

LIVERPOOL	SOUTHMPTN
Grobbelaar	Burridge
Gillespie	Forrest
Ablett	Statham
Nicol	Case
Spackman	Moore
Hansen	Bond
Beardsley	R. Wallace
Aldridge	Baker
Houghton	Clarke
Barnes	Townsend
McMahon	D. Wallace

SUBSTITUTES:
Whelan	Cockerill
Johnston	Hobson

▶ *Our celebration group on championship presentation day at Anfield. Back row (left to right): Me sharing a joke with trainer Roy Evans, Kevin MacDonald, Barry Venison, Jan Molby, Ronnie Whelan, Mike Hooper, John Barnes, Craig Johnston, Nigel Spackman, Gary Gillespie, Bruce Grobbelaar, coach Ronnie Moran, chairman John Smith, Football League secretary Graham Kelly, Barclays Bank chairman John Quinton. Front row (left to right): Jim Beglin, John Aldridge, Steve McMahon, Peter Beardsley, Alan Hansen, Steve Nicol, Ray Houghton, Gary Ablett.*

▶ *Happy moments with my wife Marina and family and the championship trophy at Anfield after the presentation which preceded our home game against Southampton.*

▼ *A great captain with a great prize: Alan Hansen holds aloft the League championship trophy.*

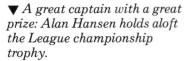

Our performance will be forgotten sooner than that but the occasion was one to cherish and I was delighted to see Alan Hansen holding aloft the championship trophy, a fitting honour for a great player who has become a great captain. I don't think his part in our success at Liverpool has been highlighted sufficiently since I became manager. When he received the old championship trophy today he dropped the lid. That is about the only thing he has done wrong all season and I am sure the public will give him a tremendous salute in his testimonial match between Liverpool and England, which has been rescheduled to take place at Anfield on Monday, 16 May – two days after the FA Cup Final – because of our match with Luton next Monday.

Shortly after I was appointed manager I had to make a decision about the captaincy and because I knew Alan so well I had no hesitation in asking him to be skipper in succession to Phil Neal. I knew he had all the qualities. I knew what to expect from him and he has more than fulfilled those expectations. He is a credit to himself and the club, and the players respect and trust him as much as I and everyone else at Anfield does. When we did the Double in 1986 Alan, as captain, did not get the recognition he deserved because the blaze of publicity was centred on me as player-manager. But the part he played in that achievement was massive, as it has been this season in which we have won the title and are now attempting to complete an unprecedented second League and FA Cup double.

During the season many things have been said and written about Alan's knee condition, much of it dramatized beyond belief. He has got a knee problem but it is nothing like as serious as it has been made out to be. Does he look like a player constantly in agony? Judged on performances, he has got to be the fittest man at the club, and he has not missed a match for us this season.

Tuesday, 3 May: UEFA caused a stir today by passing a rule stipulating that from 1990-91 only four foreign players per team would be allowed in their club competitions – and that Scots, Welsh and Irish players would be considered foreign in English sides, with the opposite applying in the other three cases. If it became effective today it would mean that for European games we could choose only four from Bruce Grobbelaar, Steve Nicol, Alan Hansen, Gary Gillespie, Ray Houghton, John Aldridge, Ronnie Whelan, Jan Molby, Kevin MacDonald and myself.

I cannot see this rule becoming a reality because lawyers have swiftly expressed their view that it contravenes the Treaty of Rome which enshrines the free movement of trade and labour in Europe. Anyway, at present, from Liverpool's point of view, it is totally hypothetical. English clubs are still suspended from UEFA competitions and once that is lifted we have to serve a further ban of three seasons in which we technically qualify for Europe.

Much more relevant to Liverpool FC was our left-back Jim Beglin's playing comeback tonight after breaking his left leg in the Littlewoods Cup game at Everton way back in January last year. Jim splashed over the waterlogged Anfield pitch – hit by a pre-match cloudburst – to help our reserves to a 3-0 Central League victory over Grimsby in his first match action since being carried off at Goodison sixteen months ago. He completed the match without any problems and the fact that his return has come just a little too late to give him a chance of making the Republic of Ireland's European Championship squad for West Germany this summer will not be too much of a regret for him.

Saturday, 7 May: Our lads produced an absolutely stunning performance at Hillsborough today to beat Sheffield Wednesday 5-1. It equalled our highest score of the season and we also hit the woodwork twice and went close with many

SHEFFIELD WEDNESDAY **LIVERPOOL**

First Division	**Hillsborough**
7 May	**35,893**

SHEFFIELD 1 (Hirst)

LIVERPOOL 5 (Johnston 2, Barnes, Beardsley 2)

SHEFFIELD	LIVERPOOL
Pressman	Grobbelaar
Sterland	Gillespie
Worthington	Ablett
Madden	Nicol
May	Spackman
Proctor	Hansen
West	Beardsley
Megson	Johnston
Chapman	Houghton
Hirst	Barnes
Jonsson	McMahon

SUBSTITUTES:

Fee	Whelan
Galvin	Molby

▶ *Peter Beardsley moves in,*
watched by Steve McMahon,
Gary Ablett and Sheffield
Wednesday's Tony Galvin,
during our 5-1 win at
Hillsborough.

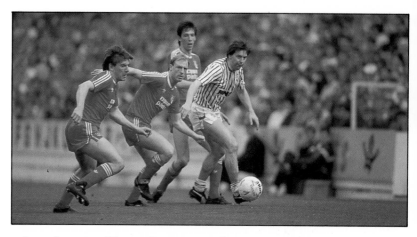

other chances. From the aspect of creating scoring opportunities it was our finest display of the season.

We were without our top scorer John Aldridge today. He has a bruised foot and rather than take any risks with him we left him out and used Craig Johnston in a central attacking role with Jan Molby and Ronnie Whelan as substitutes. We had missed several chances before Craig put us ahead after 31 minutes with the first of his two goals in the match. He scored with a powerful low shot after taking a pass from Peter Beardsley and five minutes later John Barnes made it 2-0, having been sent away by Gary Ablett's pass.

As another precaution we decided not to send out Alan Hansen for the second half. He has a slight thigh strain and there was no point in risking anything worse. So Jan Molby, who is in Denmark's squad for next week's friendly in Hungary, took over his role at centre-back alongside Gary Gillespie and played superbly, spraying the ball around and dictating the course of the game. We also sent on Ronnie Whelan in place of Steve McMahon in the 65th minute and both he and Ray Houghton had shots hit the post before Peter Beardsley scored in the 85th and 86th minutes. His first was accurately placed inside Wednesday keeper Kevin Pressman's right-hand upright and he lobbed the second over Pressman. They were two marvellous examples of Peter's skills which had Wednesday's own Kop fans enthusiastically applauding. That speaks volumes for the home supporters, especially in a day and age when football followers are constantly criticized.

Even with just a couple of minutes of the game left there was more action to come for the crowd of almost 36,000, swollen by a large contingent of our own supporters who had crossed the Pennines to give us great encouragement. David Hirst nipped in to pull a goal back for Wednesday but our lads responded by going upfield to make it 5-1 through Craig

Johnston's shot. The quality of our display was emphasized by the actions of Wednesday manager Howard Wilkinson and his assistant Peter Eustace who stood at the end and warmly applauded our lads off the pitch.

Monday, 9 May: I am beginning to have a sneaking suspicion that my decisions about when to send the Dalglish legs into first-team action are less than inspired. In March I went on for the last three minutes against Wimbledon – and we conceded a goal! Even worse, in tonight's home game against Luton I replaced Craig Johnston in the 62nd minute and we proceeded to lose *two* players.

Ten minutes after my entry as substitute, Gary Gillespie

▲ *Shaking hands with Craig Johnston when I replace him as a substitute against Luton.*

◄ *Gary Gillespie (standing) and Nigel Spackman, on the ground, receive treatment after suffering head wounds in their collision during the home match with Luton.*

◄ *John Aldridge's spectacular goal.*

LIVERPOOL   **LUTON TOWN**

First Division	**Anfield**
9 May	**30,374**

LIVERPOOL 1 (Aldridge)

LUTON 1 (Oldfield)

LIVERPOOL	LUTON
Grobbelaar	Dibble
Gillespie	Breacker
Ablett	R. Johnson
Nicol	Grimes
Spackman	Foster
Whelan	M. Johnson
Johnston	Wilson
Aldridge	Allinson
Houghton	Oldfield
Barnes	Preece
McMahon	Black

SUBSTITUTES:

Dalglish	Cobb
MacDonald	James

and Nigel Spackman went up together for a high ball, clashed heads and had to go off for stitches in wounds above their eyes. It reduced us to ten men, with Kevin MacDonald coming on as our second substitute to make his first Liverpool senior appearance since September 1986, when he broke his left leg at Southampton. The injuries to Gary and Nigel are things you can do without at any time. But in FA Cup Final week they are even more worrying and both lads were sent to a nursing home overnight for observation. Their collision overshadowed the match which we drew 1-1, a disappointing conclusion to our exciting and rewarding League season.

Before the game we received the PFA's Fair Play Trophy for collecting the least number of disciplinary points. We had only 35 against our name compared to next-best Nottingham Forest with 61 and Blackburn Rovers who collected 76. The trophy – and a cheque for £2000 to be used to provide tickets for disabled and disadvantaged children – was presented by PFA secretary Gordon Taylor to our skipper Alan Hansen. It was pleasing and a tribute to the lads to hear Gordon say: 'I'm delighted that the most successful team in the country has won this award. It proves you can be successful by playing within the laws of the game.'

After the presentation, Alan had the rare experience of *watching* Liverpool play, because we decided not to risk him while he was nursing a thigh strain. It ended his ever-present record this season and gave Steve Nicol the distinction of being the only player in the squad not to have missed a match. And tonight we made Steve skipper. We also gave Peter Beardsley a breather and pushed Ray Houghton forward in his place alongside John Aldridge, who was back after missing the Sheffield Wednesday match with a bruised foot. Ronnie Whelan and Craig Johnston both slotted into midfield.

The first corner of the match after 17 minutes brought our goal when Craig Johnston's flick header from Ray Houghton's flag kick allowed John Aldridge to score his twenty-ninth goal of the season with a spectacular overhead kick past Andy Dibble. But on the half-hour Luton were level. Rob Johnson's forward pass found David Oldfield and the nineteen-year-old, taking over from Mick Harford in attack, showed impressive pace to get past our defence and score. As well as Harford, Mal Donaghy and Ricky Hill, Brian and Mark Stein were also missing from the team that won the Littlewoods Cup by beating Arsenal at Wembley last month. One of their heroes that day, goalkeeper Dibble, produced another fine save tonight by blocking Craig Johnston's close-range shot, just before I went on as a substitute, and Luton had a chance to go ahead when Oldfield burst through but was denied by a fine tackle from Gary Ablett.

In the second half we switched John Barnes into a central attacking role with Ray Houghton reverting to midfield. But we failed to bring down the curtain on our League campaign with victory, as we would have liked. Our First Division season overall, though, has been truly memorable and although we have only equalled Everton's ninety-point record First Division total set in 1985 they played forty-two games to our forty. Our two defeats – to Everton and Nottingham Forest – equals the modern First Division record established by Leeds in 1968-69 when they played two more games than we have this season. One more accolade the whole club and its fans can be proud of is that for the first time since 1972 Liverpool are the best supported club in the Football League, our average home attendance of 39,657 surpassing Manchester United's. Although we draw on a wide radius of support, many of the people who have kept Anfield's turnstiles clicking live on Merseyside, which is hardly the most affluent area in the country. So, on behalf of everyone at Anfield, a sincere thank you for your tremendous loyalty, support and encouragement.

Tuesday, 10 May: Gary Gillespie and Nigel Spackman were allowed home today after their night in hospital following their clash of heads which meant they had to have six stitches each in wounds above their eyes. I am a bit pessimistic about their chances for Wembley, although we still have four days to go. If my worst fears are confirmed it will complete an agonizing personal double for Gary, who was ruled out of our last FA Cup Final, against Everton in 1986, because of a stomach virus.

Ironically, Jan Molby played only 45 minutes for Denmark tonight in their friendly with Hungary in Budapest. If he had not gone with Denmark he might well have played in central defence for us against Luton and the clash of heads between Gary and Nigel would never have happened.

Wednesday, 11 May: I received a telephone call at home tonight from Craig Johnston to tell me that a national newspaper is to run a first-person article by him tomorrow in which he says he intends to quit football and return to Australia when this season is over. It was a shock, to say the least. According to Craig, he had agreed to do it originally on the understanding that it would not appear until after the Cup Final. But, in my view, he should not have gone near the newspapers until after Wembley to prevent any possibility of this happening. He is entitled to his point of view and, obviously, his own future is up to him. You have to respect that. But I also have the responsibility to Liverpool FC to consider as my first priority and nothing will be allowed to interfere with the match we have coming up against Wimbledon on Saturday.

Thursday, 12 May: Craig's public declaration attracted a welter of Press, radio and TV representatives to Anfield today. I had a face-to-face discussion with him about the matter which I prefer to remain between him and me. Craig also had a talk with our chief executive Peter Robinson, who made a public statement that as Craig has another year of his club contract to run he would be in breach of contract if he did not return to pre-season training in July and the club would then consult the Professional Footballers Association about what course of action to take. It remains to be seen what the outcome will be. All I am concerned about right now is Saturday's match. Craig will be in or out of our thirteen at Wembley for no other reason than I think it is the best selection decision on the day and not through any personal reaction by me to his newspaper story.

I included Craig, as well as Gary Gillespie and Nigel Spackman, in our eighteen-man squad to travel south today. As Craig has had enough publicity exposure, and Gary and Nigel had injuries, I saw no point in them being featured in newspaper or TV photographs, so we hustled all three into the team bus by the emergency exit to escape media attention when we left Anfield for our hotel. The squad comprises the eleven who started Monday's match against Luton plus Peter Beardsley, Alan Hansen, Kevin MacDonald, myself, Alex Watson, Mike Hooper and Jan Molby. Barry Venison and Jim Beglin also travelled with us, Jim for the first time since breaking his leg against Everton last season and it was very satisfying to have him with us after such a long absence.

After checking into our hotel tonight, John Barnes went through to London to receive his Footballer of the Year Award from the Football Writers Association at their annual presentation dinner.

Friday, 13 May: This time it was my task to travel to the capital from our headquarters to be presented with the Manager of the Year Award at the Bells Whisky lunch in a London hotel. It was the second time in three seasons I have had the honour of receiving this award but I did so in the belief that it is only a reflection of the overall efforts of the club. I

▼ *John Barnes after receiving the Footballer of the Year trophy from the Football Writers Association.*

told the luncheon guests: 'At the start of the season we lost Ian Rush and I gave the directors the names of the players to replace him and they backed me. My name is on this award but I am only a substitute. It could easily read Liverpool FC.'

The last time I received this award, before our FA Cup Final against Everton in 1986, I was slated by certain quarters of the media for being presented with the trophy before the lunch and then returning to the team hotel. This time I stayed for the lunch and sat at the same table as Bobby Gould, manager of Wimbledon. But on the way back to our hotel I could not help ponder on whether players – or player-managers like myself – are doing the right thing by their clubs in attending presentation functions in the immediate build-up to a Cup Final as John Barnes and I have done. I say this with absolutely no disrespect to either the FWA or Bells, who have honoured us with their awards. But Thursday evening and Friday lunchtime are very important stages of the approach to the Cup Final and perhaps switching the presentation functions to the following week or bringing them forward a day or two would be better for the award winners who are with a club participating in the Final.

Saturday, 14 May: Our attempt to re-write football's record books and become the first club in the history of the game in England to win the League and FA Cup double twice ended in Wembley disappointment. My fears earlier in the week that neither Gary Gillespie nor Nigel Spackman would be available for selection were dispelled at the hotel when Ronnie Moran and Roy Evans returned from a heading session with the two lads, whose wounds had been padded, to report that they had come through with no problems. So I decided to include them both in my starting line-up.

We left our Watford hotel having received a greetings message from Frank Sinatra which read: 'All good wishes for the League and Cup double.' Unfortunately, we were not totally on song during the game. But while everyone in our camp was disappointed with the performance as well as the 1-0 defeat we played well enough not to have lost. Apart from a second-half penalty I don't think we got one bounce of the ball in the whole game which, ultimately, was won and lost in two minutes before the interval.

In the 34th minute Peter Beardsley had shrugged off an illegal challenge by Andy Thorn to go on and 'chip' Wimbledon's goalkeeping captain Dave Beasant to put the ball in the net. Peter said he never heard referee Brian Hill

▲ *A proud moment for me and Liverpool FC following the presentation of the Bells Manager of the Year Award.*

LIVERPOOL	WIMBLEDON
FA Cup Final	**Wembley**
14 May	**98,203**
LIVERPOOL 0	
WIMBLEDON 1 (Sanchez)	
LIVERPOOL	WIMBLEDON
Grobbelaar	Beasant
Gillespie	Goodyear
Ablett	Phelan
Nicol	Jones
Spackman	Young
Hansen	Thorn
Beardsley	Gibson
Aldridge	Cork
Houghton	Fashanu
Barnes	Sanchez
McMahon	Wise
SUBSTITUTES:	
Johnston	Scales
Molby	Cunningham

▶ *Nigel Spackman sports a natty line in head-bands to protect his wound in the FA Cup Final against Wimbledon at Wembley.*

▶ *Meeting the Princess of Wales at Wembley before the FA Cup Final.*

▶ *One of the Final's crucial moments as Wimbledon's goalkeeping captain Dave Beasant saves John Aldridge's penalty.*

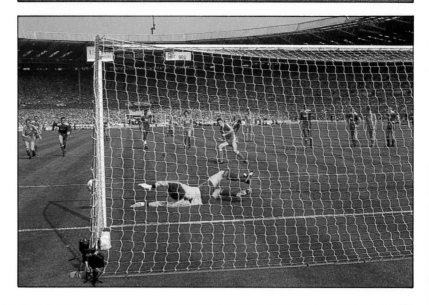

◀ *Urging on the lads from the Wembley bench during the Final.*

◀ *Our tour of Liverpool the day after our Wembley disappointment restored our smiles, because our loyal supporters gave us a wonderful ovation as we took the League championship trophy around the city on our open-top bus.*

blow his whistle and Beasant surely did not hear it otherwise he would not have dived to try to stop Peter putting the ball in. But the referee wiped off the 'goal', pulled play back for the free kick and after it had been cleared Wimbledon went downfield and took the lead. George Tyson, the well-known referee this time officiating as a linesman, flagged for a free kick to Wimbledon after deciding that Steve Nicol had pulled back Terry Phelan. Dennis Wise took the kick, Lawrie Sanchez headed it and we were 1-0 down, although I did not have a clue who had scored the goal until well after the match. The identity of the scorer was not that important to me, anyway.

I did not watch television recordings of the game so I cannot talk with any authority about the merits or otherwise of our penalty award on the hour. All I know is that the referee gave it when John Aldridge fell in the box after a tussle with Clive

Goodyear. We had been planning to take John off before that incident so his eventual substitution by Craig Johnston four minutes after his penalty kick had been saved by Beasant was no reflection on what happened. We also sent on Jan Molby in place of Nigel Spackman to use up all our options and go for broke. But we failed in our task of trying to break down Wimbledon who either sat back or were pushed back after scoring their goal. John Aldridge took the burden of our defeat on his own shoulders but he should not reproach himself in any way. He got the penalty on target but it was saved, the first time he has failed to score from the spot in twelve attempts for Liverpool. He has scored some crucial goals for us, including both – one a penalty – in our semi-final win over Nottingham Forest. Naturally, he was disappointed, just like Peter Beardsley, who might have put us on the road to victory if a decision had gone for us, and everyone else in the squad.

I will never forget the look of deep disappointment etched on the face of my eleven-year-old son Paul at the end as he sat next to my wife Marina. It was a feeling shared by the whole Liverpool camp and the lads, as good professionals, know they could have played better.

Some of the media expressed the view this morning that we had to win for the sake of English football. It makes a change from people saying that we win too much! So let's get it straight. We went to Wembley to try to win the Cup for Liverpool, in the way we thought best. Wimbledon did the same and they had every right to be there. They also have a right to hold up the FA Cup because they beat us 1-0.

▼ *Bruce Grobbelaar shouting instructions during the Final.*

Monday, 16 May: I am angry at today's newspaper column by Emlyn Hughes in which he makes some outrageous comments about Alan Hansen, whose testimonial match at Anfield tonight was a marvellous occasion. Under a headline pronouncing 'Hansen Must Go', Hughes claims that Alan's knee problem has taken the edge off his game. That is absolute nonsense. There has been no secret about Alan's persistent knee problem but there has been no secret either about the marvellous quality of his performances. It has been evident match after match but apparently not so evident to Emlyn Hughes. I repeat that Alan Hansen is a great captain and a great player, better than most who have no knee problems. As a former Liverpool captain, Hughes should know better than to come out in the media with the type of rubbish he is talking today when he says 'Hansen has been the rock at the back for Liverpool for so long. Now that rock is

◀ *A special salute to our skipper Alan Hansen from the crowd and the players as he steps out for his testimonial match between Liverpool and England.*

beginning to crumble.' I remember Hughes applying a canister of hot spray to his own knee before going out for training but nobody made a public song and dance about that fact. The last time he came to a match at Anfield he did not even pop downstairs to say hello to people he worked with at Liverpool for so many years, people with whom he shared so many great and successful moments. After this outburst today I do not think he would be made very welcome if he showed his face again.

The Liverpool fans certainly showed the high esteem in which they hold Alan when more than 31,000 turned out tonight for his testimonial against an England team selected by Bobby Robson, a match we won 3-2 thanks to two goals from a certain Ian Rush and another from Ronnie Whelan. Our supporters, who turned out in their thousands to welcome us home yesterday, showed why they are the best in the business and how much they feel for Liverpool by saluting Alan Hansen, chanting John Aldridge's name and giving a great welcome back to Rushie.

I got a job I had not bargained for tonight. The matter of team selection was originally supposed to be Alan's, because it was his night. But he bottled that one and asked me to pick the side! Some of our changes from Saturday were enforced ones because Steve Nicol is away with Scotland, preparing for tomorrow's Rous Cup game against Colombia, and Gary Gillespie is also unavailable after withdrawing from the Scottish squad suffering after-effects of his head wound. So Nigel Spackman switched to right-back and Jan Molby came into the back four alongside Alan. And, bearing in mind Craig Johnston's public declaration last week that he intends to quit football and return to Australia, I named him in the team

LIVERPOOL	ENGLAND XI
Alan Hansen Testimonial	**Anfield**
16 May	**31,552**

LIVERPOOL 3 (Whelan, Rush 2)

ENGLAND 2 (Harford, Waddle)

LIVERPOOL	ENGLAND
Grobbelaar	Shilton
Spackman	Stevens
Ablett	Sansom
Molby	Reid
Whelan	Watson
Hansen	Wright
Beardsley	Steven
Aldridge	S. Robson
Johnston	Harford
Barnes	Waddle
McMahon	Hodge

SUBSTITUTES:	
Rush	Webb
Dalglish	Woods
Houghton	Adams
Watson	
Staunton	

to give our fans a last chance to see him in action before replacing him for the second half with Ray Houghton.

During the first half Rushie went on in place of Peter Beardsley and the place erupted to welcome back their former hero who had made the trip from Italy to play in Alan's game after appearing for Juventus yesterday. At half-time I decided to give the Dalglish legs another run-out and roll back the years by partnering Rushie up front. I went on instead of John Aldridge for the second half and it was nice to be reunited once again with Rushie and even nicer to help the great man pop in a couple of goals. They came after Rushie himself had laid on the chance for Ronnie Whelan to equalize England's first-half goal from Mick Harford. Chris Waddle scored their other one between Rushie's brace which was crowned by the Kop chanting 'Come back home', underlining that he is still a part of them. It was a memorable evening and I doubt if one person left the ground at the end until Alan Hansen had completed his lap of the pitch.

Tonight was the last time our lads will have the name Crown Paints on their jerseys. The conclusion of their sponsorship ends a very happy and successful six-year association with the club. On behalf of the players and staff, and I know the club as a whole, I would like to thank them and look forward to a similar relationship with our new sponsors Candy.

Saturday, 21 May: What a pleasing way to round off the season – a run-out at Wembley, victory over the English and all in a good cause! The occasion was a seven-a-side charity match between Old England and Old Scotland, preceding the Rous Cup game between the countries. It was in aid of the Lee Smith Research Foundation on behalf of the Institute of Child Health at Great Ormond Street Hospital, funding the vital research into leukaemia and related illnesses, and I am glad to report that our little bit of fun raised around £25,000 to help swell the coffers.

Paul Mariner assembled an England team which had Phil Parkes in goal and an outfield of Mick Mills, Dave Watson, Alan Ball, Trevor Brooking, Bobby Moore and Paul himself. I had the pleasure of making a few telephone calls to recruit a side comprising goalkeeper Bryan Gunn – as he is Norwich City's current First Division keeper he is excused the title 'old'! – Frankie Gray, Graeme Souness, Danny McGrain, John Wark, myself and the one and only Rod Stewart.

Modesty almost forbids me to record that yours truly put our side one goal up before I had the pleasure of combining

◀ *Seven up at Wembley — that's me on the left with the rest of the 'Old Scotland' seven-a-side team before our win over 'Old England' in a charity match at Wembley which was a pipe-opener to the Rous Cup game between the countries. My team-mates are Danny McGrain, John Wark, Rod Stewart, Graeme Souness, Bryan Gunn and Frankie Gray; and my eleven-year-old son Paul got his chance to be a Wembley mascot!*

with Mr Stewart, who made it 2-0. And Frankie Gray, taking advantage of a Graeme Souness pass, completed a famous victory by making it 3-0.

But if that was an enjoyable experience, the sight of fighting on the Wembley terracing between English and Scottish supporters was saddening. Sports Minister Colin Moynihan has responded by implying that the British Government cannot give UEFA the guarantee they want about the behaviour of English fans for their consideration in lifting the general European ban on English clubs. But no government, in any country, can give guarantees like that. There are problems with hooligan elements amongst supporters in almost every country, but English football's problem is that our thugs export their violence.

The ugly scenes at Wembley were caused by a lack of segregation, which was perhaps the biggest single factor in the tragedy at our 1985 European Cup Final against Juventus in Brussels. Segregation must surely be a fundamental bottom line in the battle to prevent football violence. So must the ability of the police to nip potential problems in the bud, just as the Glasgow police did last year when a band of English fans was rounded up and sent straight back home. If the Wembley fighting has dispelled the last hope for English clubs being back in UEFA competitions next season it would be a shame after all the efforts, in concert with local authorities and police forces, they have made.

After Wembley, there has been immediate talk, even from the Sports Minister himself, of scrapping the England v Scotland fixture. I think such talk is premature and some cool thinking needs to be done. This fixture has great tradition, is a highlight of the football calendar on both sides of the border and both countries and their players look forward to it with relish each season. Obviously games cannot go on at all costs, but let us hope some solution can be found. Today's latest match in the series which stretches back to 1872 offered proof of the saying that a week is a long time in football.

Last Saturday, Peter Beardsley had the agonizing experience of having his FA Cup Final 'goal' disallowed by the referee. Today his almost identical strike against Scotland's Jim Leighton counted – and Peter's 11th-minute goal, which John Barnes helped create, gave England a deserved 1-0 victory. The decision to chalk off Peter's strike a week ago was a costly one for us because the first goal is always important, especially in a game like that, and our 1-0 defeat was our biggest disappointment of the season. But we reached the Final and if somebody had asked me a year ago about what we wanted from the season I would have settled for the League championship, even though you get the same thrill at winning a cup over a few games as the title over forty.

Right from the end of last season we had to get used to the fact that Ian Rush had gone. I signed the players I told our board I wanted and they, and the rest of the lads, responded superbly. Some people now talk about this team with the benefit of hindsight. But when we signed the new players, John Barnes and Peter Beardsley following John Aldridge and Nigel Spackman and preceding Ray Houghton, we did not have the benefit of hindsight. We had to back our judgment.

By the time our lads lost their first League game – at Everton in March – a lot of jealousy had developed about our unbeaten run and our 1-0 defeat at Goodison gave many people a lot of pleasure. Critics had written that it was bad for English football that one team should dominate. But why should we lower our standards? Surely it is up to other clubs to raise theirs?

The players shrugged off that disappointment and went on to clinch the championship in style and put another feather in their caps by becoming the country's best-supported team. Now we are looking forward to the new season with the same determined attitude but not necessarily exactly the same set of players or the same style of play. We are always looking at the chance of improving the squad, which is not to say we are unhappy with the players we have. But that process of searching for talent is a continuous one at Anfield. And now that other teams have had a look at us during the past season we will have to be ready to change our pattern of play if need be to face the challenges ahead.

Once upon a time, Liverpool's maxim at the start of each

season used to be a statement of intent to clinch a European qualifying place for the following campaign. Our European suspension has banished all that. Now we approach a new season with the aim of being in the following year's Charity Shield which, to all intents and purposes, means winning either the League or FA Cup. But, once again, we will be trying to win both of them as well as the Littlewoods Cup. It is unlikely that we will win all three domestic trophies but we did a treble, including the European Cup, under Joe Fagan's management, so a domestic threesome is possible. Likewise, although it is improbable, you have to believe you can complete a First Division programme unbeaten. We lost just twice in forty League games during the past season, so a season undefeated is not beyond the bounds of possibility. One thing is certain. Our appetite for success is unsatiable, our desire undiminished by past triumphs. This season has been deeply memorable. Now here's to the next one!

DIVISION ONE

Final table

	P	W	D	L	F	A	Pts
Liverpool	**40**	**26**	**12**	**2**	**87**	**24**	**90**
Man Utd	40	23	12	5	71	38	81
Nottm For	40	20	13	7	67	39	73
Everton	40	19	13	8	53	27	70
QPR	40	19	10	11	48	38	67
Arsenal	40	18	12	10	58	39	66
Wimbledon	40	14	15	11	58	47	57
Newcastle	40	14	14	12	55	53	56
Luton	40	14	11	15	57	58	53
Coventry	40	13	14	13	46	53	53
Sheff Wed	40	15	8	17	52	66	53
Southmptn	40	12	14	14	49	53	50
Tottenham	40	12	11	17	38	48	47
Norwich	40	12	9	19	40	52	45
Derby	40	10	13	17	35	45	43
West Ham	40	9	15	16	40	52	42
Charlton	40	9	15	16	38	52	42
Chelsea	40	9	15	16	50	68	42
Portsmth	40	7	14	19	36	66	35
Watford	40	7	11	22	27	51	32
Oxford	40	6	13	21	44	80	31

Chelsea relegated after losing 2-1 on aggregate to Middlesbrough in First/Second Division play-offs. Middlesbrough promoted with Millwall and Aston Villa.

STATISTICS

Player	League		FA Cup		Lwoods Cup		Totals	
	A	G	A	G	A	G	A	G
Bruce Grobbelaar	38	0	5	0	3	0	46	0
Steve Nicol	40	6	7	0	3	1	50	7
Barry Venison	19	0	1	0	2	0	22	0
Gary Gillespie	35	4	5	0	2	0	42	4
Ronnie Whelan	28	1	2	0	3	0	33	1
Alan Hansen	39	1	7	0	3	0	49	1
Peter Beardsley	38	15	7	3	3	0	48	18
Craig Johnston	29	5	4	1	2	0	35	6
John Aldridge	36	26	6	2	3	1	45	29
Steve McMahon	40	9	7	0	2	0	49	9
John Barnes	38	15	7	2	3	0	48	17
Paul Walsh	8	0	0	0	1	0	9	0
Nigel Spackman	27	0	5	0	1	0	33	0
John Wark	1	0	0	0	1	0	2	0
Mark Lawrenson	14	0	2	0	3	0	19	0
Ray Houghton	28	5	7	2	0	0	35	7
Jan Molby	7	0	1	0	0	0	8	0
Gary Ablett	17	0	5	0	0	0	22	0
Mike Hooper	2	0	2	0	0	0	4	0
Alex Watson	2	0	0	0	0	0	2	0
Kenny Dalglish	2	0	0	0	0	0	2	0
Kevin MacDonald	1	0	0	0	0	0	1	0
Goal totals:		87		10		2		99

Note: Players' appearance figures A include those made as substitute. G – goals.

Highest score: 5 (5-0 v. Nottingham Forest (home), First Division, 13 April, 1988; 5-1 v. Sheffield Wednesday (away), First Division, 7 May, 1988)

Highest home attendance: 44,798 (v. Tottenham, First Division, 23 April, 1988)

Average home League attendance: 39,657